'This book is a valuable text, providing helpful insights into areas that need to be considered by those entering higher education as mature students. The book is accessibly written and covers both practical and academic issues to support mature students prior to, during, and at the end of their higher education study. As well as discussing some common concerns mature students may have prior to entering study, the book also provides practical guidance and suggests techniques to support the development of study skills, academic writing and criticality, all of which are essential for students to succeed in higher education.'

Carol Robinson, *Professor of Children's Rights and Co-director of Postgraduate Research, Institute of Education, University of Strathclyde*

The Mature Student's Companion for Successful Undergraduate Study

A guiding resource and supportive companion, this book is designed for mature individuals intending to undertake an undergraduate degree.

Comprehensively yet succinctly covering all of the knowledge and skills expected when studying at university, it recognises that mature students face a variety of obstacles that have to be carefully circumnavigated and that often, the support for doing this is difficult to find in one place. With a wealth of practical strategies for developing a range of key study skills, whilst, at the same time, addressing the difficulties people face in preparing for the numerous changes that university study can bring, this key text highlights to the reader the significance of individual strengths obtained from life experiences, and demonstrates their importance and utility in learning as a mature student.

Packed full of activities to support development and case studies to exemplify a range of situations, this is a must-read for anyone looking to undertake an undergraduate degree as a mature student.

David Allan is Reader in Professional Education and Learning at Edge Hill University, UK where he teaches on a BA and an MA and supervises PhD students, all studying in the field of Education.

Routledge Study Skills

The Mature Student's Companion for Successful Undergraduate Study
David Allan

The Mature Student's Guide to Completing a Doctorate
Sinéad Hewson

The Student Wellbeing Toolkit
Preparing for Life at College, University and Beyond
Camila Devis-Rozental

Writing a Postgraduate Thesis or Dissertation
Tools for Success
Michael Hammond

Studying Online
Succeeding through Distance Learning at University
Graham Jones

For more information about this series, please visit: https://www.routledge.com/Routledge-Study-Skills/book-series/ROUTLEDGESS

The Mature Student's Companion for Successful Undergraduate Study

David Allan

LONDON AND NEW YORK

Designed cover image: © Getty Images

First published 2025
by Routledge
4 Park Square, Milton Park, Abingdon, Oxon OX14 4RN

and by Routledge
605 Third Avenue, New York, NY 10158

Routledge is an imprint of the Taylor & Francis Group, an informa business

© 2025 David Allan

The right of David Allan to be identified as author of this work has been asserted in accordance with sections 77 and 78 of the Copyright, Designs and Patents Act 1988.

All rights reserved. No part of this book may be reprinted or reproduced or utilised in any form or by any electronic, mechanical, or other means, now known or hereafter invented, including photocopying and recording, or in any information storage or retrieval system, without permission in writing from the publishers.

Trademark notice: Product or corporate names may be trademarks or registered trademarks, and are used only for identification and explanation without intent to infringe.

British Library Cataloguing-in-Publication Data
A catalogue record for this book is available from the British Library

Library of Congress Cataloging-in-Publication Data
Names: Allan, David (College teacher), author.
Title: The mature student's companion for successful undergraduate study / David Allan.
Description: Abingdon, Oxon; New York, NY: Routledge, 2025. | Series: Routledge study skills | Includes bibliographical references and index. |
Identifiers: LCCN 2024061021 (print) | LCCN 2024061022 (ebook) | ISBN 9781032619231 (hardback) | ISBN 9781032619248 (paperback) | ISBN 9781032619255 (ebook)
Subjects: LCSH: Adult education. | Adult college students. | Older people–Education (Higher) | Motivation in adult education.
Classification: LCC LC5215 .A377 2025 (print) | LCC LC5215 (ebook) | DDC 378.1/9824–dc23/eng/20250225
LC record available at https://lccn.loc.gov/2024061021
LC ebook record available at https://lccn.loc.gov/2024061022

ISBN: 978-1-032-61923-1 (hbk)
ISBN: 978-1-032-61924-8 (pbk)
ISBN: 978-1-032-61925-5 (ebk)

DOI: 10.4324/9781032619255

Typeset in Warnock Pro
by SPi Technologies India Pvt Ltd (Straive)

This book is dedicated to my wife, Venetia, and my children: Daniel, Jamie, Sophie and Harry. I would particularly like to thank my wife for her support throughout the writing.

Contents

List of Illustrations x

▶ 1 **What It Means to Be a Mature Student** 1

▶ 2 **Developing Your Study Skills** 18

▶ 3 **Time Management and Organisational Skills** 33

▶ 4 **Autonomy and Being an Independent Learner** 49

▶ 5 **The Art of Note-Taking** 62

▶ 6 **How to Engage in Critical Reading** 82

▶ 7 **Constructing an Argument** 93

▶ 8 **Academic Writing** 107

▶ 9 **Referencing** 120

▶ 10 **Revising and Polishing Your Writing** 132

▶ 11 **Making the Most of Your Personal Tutor** 144

▶ 12 **Bon Voyage** 154

Index 157

Illustrations

FIGURES

Figure 2.1	File Management	30
Figure 5.1	Recording your notes	70

TABLES

Table 1.1	SWOT Analysis	4
Table 3.1	Example Weekly Timetable	36
Table 3.2	Example Termly Plan	43
Table 5.1	Notetaking methods	72
Table 7.1	Point, evidence, explain	95
Table 8.1	Writing approaches	110
Table 9.1	Questions for including citations	130
Table 11.1	Personal tutorial schedule	150

BOXES

Box 1.1	Activity	14
Box 5.1	Cognitive dissonance and smoking	65
Box 6.1	FAQs	87

1 What It Means to Be a Mature Student

▶ **INTRODUCTION**

Congratulations on deciding to become a student of higher education. This was perhaps not an easy decision to make but hopefully it will be the right one for you and thus enable you to fulfil your dreams. You may be nervous about studying again – perhaps you have had a long break and worked in various jobs, maybe even another profession – but you should be at ease with the thought that as a mature student you have a lot to offer when studying in higher education. This includes your life experience, focus and determination, and capacity to commit to your studies. And you are certainly not alone as a mature student. Every year, tens of thousands of individuals across the world make the decision to return to learning, and thousands of those go on to have successful careers in their chosen field (Office for Students, 2021). Indeed, mature students constitute about '37% of all undergraduate entrants' (Hubble & Bolton, 2021, p. 3). And whilst the majority of students on full-time courses in England are younger students, for part-time undergraduate degrees mature students represent around 86% of the entrants (Office for Students, 2023).

Age is also even less of a concern when we bear in mind that older mature students perform better on average than younger mature students (Pearce, 2017). As a mature student, particularly if you have a clear idea of what you want from your degree, you are likely to be more equipped to deal with demands. However, this does not mean that you won't face challenges, and you will need to utilise these resources and push yourself so that you are fully engaged with your studies. Undertaking a degree requires great commitment on your behalf, particularly in relation to reading, note-taking, synthesizing data, forming new concepts, and writing assignments, and these will all be unpacked in this book.

In many ways, the student journey is similar for everyone, but the transition can be particularly challenging when you are a mature student. You may be returning to study because you have recently re-evaluated your ambitions, or perhaps you are about to embark on your second career. This is quite common in today's society. Indeed, the Office for National Statistics (2022) shows that the figure for 'job changers' in the UK has risen in recent years (and quite significantly since the pandemic). In the US the picture is also quite similar, with one longitudinal study noting that its participants 'held an average of 12.7 jobs from ages 18 to 56' (Bureau of Labor Statistics, 2023, p. 1). Having multiple careers is more common than you might imagine, then, and there are many reasons why people change careers. Some feel unsatisfied in their current positions, whilst others call for excitement, seeking out new and even radically different career challenges. For many, however, it is an opportunity to pursue a lifetime ambition.

To begin on your journey, then, you should think about what you hope to achieve from your studies. In this way, you can be clear about your forthcoming commitment. This will also enable you to devise a bespoke plan that can facilitate this. You may need your degree for a specific career and that is in many ways a valid reason. Going to university can mean a difference in (gross) earnings over your lifetime of between £140,000 and £240,000 (Britton et al., 2020). But what does that mean for your attitude to learning? Are you going to be fixated on just getting through? Or would you like to get more out of your studies? The purpose of HE is not to merely attain a certificate to work in a chosen field; rather, it should be a highly rewarding and individually developmental experience.

▶ LEARNING AND EDUCATION

According to Dewey (1997, p. 10), education should 'prepare the young for future responsibilities and for success in life,' whilst Cremin (1976, p. 27) holds that education is 'the deliberate, systematic, and sustained effort to transmit, provoke or acquire knowledge, values, attitudes, skills or sensibilities as well as any learning that results from the effort.' In both cases, it is viewed as a structured system of transmitting (or facilitating the construction of) knowledge. This would suggest that it is a means to a clearly defined end and, as such, is interrelated with objectives, goals and perhaps aspirations. You may have a different perspective on the purpose of education, but it is useful to ask yourself what it is and how it can work for you. For some, it is a route to employment; but higher education provides much more. It promotes intellectual growth and the expansion of the mind, and it is a mechanism for exposing yourself to challenging ideas. It can open you up to new conceptual frameworks that develop your approach to problem solving, thus helping you to deal with some of life's adversities and enabling you to see the world in a different light. Higher education is about growing your autonomy and developing metacognition (how you think about the way you think). It is thus about taking control of your learning and planning your individual journey.

Learning itself has been defined in a variety of ways, depending on the field. For instance, through a cognitive science perspective, Kirschner et al. (2006, p. 75) describes it as 'a change in long-term memory.' Perhaps more akin to the behaviourist school of thinking, however, Hilgard et al. (1961, p. 6) suggest that it is 'a relatively permanent change in behavioral potentiality that occurs as a result of reinforced practice.' Understanding learning is useful because it can help you to maximize your intellectual potential. But you are not expected to delve into the latest neuroscience debate or unpick the philosophical elements of what it means to learn. As a mature student it is in your best interest to get to know yourself more, to diagnose what methods work well for you and what pattern of learning is the most productive. In this way, you can avoid the pitfalls, such as sitting up till 4 in the morning writing an assignment when your intellectual capacity for that sort of thing may have left you way before midnight. Understanding how you work best will save you a lot of wasted time and energy, and to achieve this you will need to invest in a brief period of self-analysis.

▶ ESTABLISH YOUR FOUNDATION

In order to identify your current skillset and experience, you can conduct a short self-analysis of your current abilities. You can do this using the following SWOT (Strengths, Weaknesses, Opportunities and threats) table. To get you started, some examples have been included. And whilst you do not need to be overly detailed, you do need to attain a realistic picture of your capabilities and areas for development (Table 1.1).

When you complete this activity, you may find that some of your perceived weaknesses or threats are actually strengths. What this

TABLE 1.1 SWOT Analysis

Strengths	Weaknesses	Opportunities	Threats	Notes
E.g. 10 years' work experience in engineering firm	Length of time since last study period	Network of like-minded individuals	Finances	Use MOOCs to build on gaps in subject knowledge.
Mature approach	Academic ability	MOOCs	Confidence	
Self-motivated	Confidence and self-esteem		Family commitments	Age is a potential benefit so gap may not be a concern.
Clear in focus and aspirational			Age gap with peers	

means is that there are in fact many benefits that can be taken from these areas, and you just need to do a little recalculation. Your perception of being a mature student, for instance, might position it as a disadvantage. But the reality is that you may have quite a substantial advantage over your peers if you have a lot of experience. One of the challenges for employers today is that of graduates lacking both work and life experience (Matsouka & Mihail, 2016). As a mature student, you may possess much of this already.

Once you have completed this exercise, you can then use the information to steer your progress over the next three years. And you should update it regularly with examples, such as any courses or work placements you undertake. It is never too early to begin collating this evidence, and your SWOT document will eventually be smoothly transferred to your CV, providing an accurate representation of your skills and achievements and saving you much time later on.

▶ FITTING IN

As a mature student, you may have concerns studying alongside students who are younger than you. But higher education is a mature environment and age is often just a figure in relation to what is expected of you. You are all adults and will be treated as such. At this level, you are required to engage critically with the materials, resources, concepts and so on, which means thinking more deeply about your topic. You will engage in debates around theories and perspectives, embrace and challenge the thoughts of your peers, and present a robust defence of your own thinking. You may even be required to challenge yourself at times, so it is good to enter higher education with an open mind. In this way, you are engaging in intellectual discourse, opening yourself up to new ideas, and acknowledging that there are often many ways to address a problem. You should even be prepared to challenge the ideas of your lecturers, where appropriate. This is not disagreeing with someone for the sake of it. Rather, it requires exploring a topic in a different way – applying an alternative lens, for instance, to see what results can be obtained. Needless to say, all forms of challenging are there to progress the debate and not to arbitrarily offend or discriminate against anyone. Lecturers recognise that students may be passionate about some topical concerns so all discussions will be monitored and steered towards productive outcomes. Disagreements should be fun and interesting, and never executed in an *ad hominem* manner. That is, they should be based on the topic in hand and never personalised or intentionally aimed at the individual.

▶ WHAT TO EXPECT

You may be wondering what university study will be like. Will it be similar to your time at school, for instance, or your college experience? Will you have lectures each day of the week? You will probably find degree-level study to be widely different from your previous study, however, with contact time in the classroom varying but averaging around six to fifteen hours per week (depending on your course as some involve even more hours). This is not the extent of your weekly study, however, as you are required to invest time in addition to these hours through what is sometimes termed 'self-study' or 'independent learning.' Full-time study can generally be 30–40 hours and you will manage this time yourself. Contact time will consist of teaching through a variety of forms. Typical ones are outlined below.

Lectures

A lecture is a talk, usually one-sided, where the speaker (or lecturer) delivers information on a particular subject. For instance, the lecturer may present a theme critique a theory, or explore a topic. The lecture is used to generate interest and insight for the listener (student) and should thus be informative. The lecturer may focus on a particular assignment on the course to illustrate the detail of analysis that is needed at degree level. The lecturer may also call for some interaction, albeit this is often at a minimum as it is usually reserved for seminars and in-class teaching. The strength of the lecture lies in its capacity for the transference of expertise – i.e. a knowledgeable individual bestows some of his/her specialist knowledge upon the listener – and the potential for wide, and simultaneous, dissemination. For degree programmes, for instance, all cohorts can attend the lecture and thus benefit from the same information being presented to everyone at the same time. This varies from classroom practice where the sessions for each cohort might differ. Lectures overcome this by the approach of a single delivery. The weakness of a lecture, however, is the lack of interaction. This can result in students having difficulty in obtaining clarification in the moment, and some will switch off and may even disengage without the lecturer knowing.

Seminars

A seminar is a bespoke discussion on a chosen area and functions like a mini conference. On degree courses, it is often run in a similar manner to that of a teaching session, albeit it is designed to generate greater interaction. In a seminar, a group of individuals – e.g. a class of students and a lecturer, or facilitator – discuss a topic in depth. In this way, a seminar may immediately follow a lecture and provide the opportunity for the subject of the lecture to be further explored in the classroom. This is an opportunity to see how the ideas raised can resonate with the group.

Workshops

Workshops are similar to seminars although they tend to focus on an outcome, such as the creation of a product or an artefact, or the posing of a solution to the proposed challenge. A lecturer may initiate a workshop where something can be tested with an audience, such as a new theory or approach, and thus developed. Whereas seminars may be open-ended and merely debate the issue in hand, a workshop will attempt to bring closure to the challenge, ideally in the form of a solution.

Classroom teaching

This is often done in a similar style to that of college teaching or sixth forms but employs greater flexibility in the interactions. Discussions are open and adult-like and may even appear informal. There may be activities for the students to do and these can be undertaken individually, in pairs, or in groups. Taught sessions can be interactive and may at times require the students to formally prepare for them. An example of this would be the flipped classroom, where students are asked to engage in some preparatory work before the teaching session. For example, the students might read an article before the lesson and then prepare for a debate on the themes or ideas emerging from this reading.

Tutorials

These are often individual sessions between you and your personal tutor, albeit you may initially have a group tutorial to discuss some of the common concerns across the group. Your personal tutor is there to guide you along the process of undertaking your degree. The one-to-one nature of a typical tutorial means that you have the personalised support of a professional who can identify and address your needs beyond the acquisition of mere academic skills or subject knowledge. For a fuller description of this role, see Chapter 11.

▶ YOU AND YOUR ROLE

In addition to participating in the above, you will also be expected to contribute to classroom debates. These enable the teaching sessions to be interactive and are a necessary part of your development as a scholar. Higher education is not merely about taking down a few notes in the classroom, listening to what the experts have to say, and then writing an assignment that encompasses that experience and confirms everything your lecturer told you. It is about challenge and criticality, i.e. not accepting things on face value but requiring a deeper body of evidence and prior knowledge to substantiate an argument. Therefore, you may be asked to engage in more formal academic pursuits, such as presenting your ideas to the class or even a wider audience. In this way, you are open to the critique of the group and your peers can also see what you have presented for your assignment (a bit like reading your essay). This should not be seen as daunting, however, but empowering. Your peers should be supportive of what you do (and vice versa) and challenge your argument so that you can evidence its validity. Your time at university is focused on building your independent ability as a future scholar, and this means engaging in a variety of activities, challenging ideas and assumptions, and generally employing a critical approach.

If your fear as a mature student is that you have gaps in your learning, or that you are out of the practice of studying, there are many free online resources available that can help. One example is MOOCs (Massive Open Online Courses) (see https://www.mooc.org/) with over 3,000 study modules available. You can study for free and catch up (or get ahead) with your favourite subject. Indeed, before you begin your HE studies you might want to participate in a taster course so that you can get back into the swing of learning. This is a great confidence booster, and with such a wide variety of courses to choose from it can also be addictive. MOOCS present opportunities for those in less fortunate positions, such as those who have no means of acquiring funding. Ironically, however, the largest users of MOOCs are graduates (Christensen et al., 2013). Of course, you may wonder why you should bother with university study at all with thousands of seemingly free courses at your fingertips. But MOOCs are not a free alternative means of gaining a full degree. If you want certification, there is likely to be a fee somewhere down the line.

▶ ARTIFICIAL INTELLIGENCE

This is currently taking universities by storm and in many ways it is a concern for academia because it is very accessible, easy to use, and acceptable usage is still being demarcated. There are many uses of artificial intelligence (AI), however, and as it is topical at present it is likely that it will be discussed in some way on your course. Usually this is in the form of, 'please don't plagiarise or cheat by getting AI to write your assignment for you.' But it may also be that you are in a university that is embracing some of the strengths of AI. At present, using AI would largely be considered cheating, or plagiarising – passing work off as your own when someone (or something) else has written it. Getting AI to write something for you is plagiarism because you are not the author of that work. But in many ways, plagiarism is quite easy to do unintentionally so you should be careful to read up on the relevant academic conventions (see Chapters 7–9). For instance, if you quote a piece of writing by another author but innocently forget to include quotation marks then this would be regarded as plagiarism. Moreover, it is also possible to plagiarise yourself. Suppose you mistakenly included a large chunk of your writing from an assignment that you had previously submitted. Including that same text a second time now constitutes plagiarism. This may seem confusing as plagiarism is typically viewed as passing off someone else's work as your own, and clearly this is your own work. But it is plagiarism because you are reusing it yet simultaneously claiming it as original writing. Authors who reuse text from their previous publications are also guilty of this if they do not acknowledge the original source, i.e. cite themselves.

Despite the concerns raised by many universities, AI has many strengths. And, as mentioned earlier, some universities are embracing this. Where spellcheckers were once considered cheating, they are now accepted by many as a useful tool for assignment writing. Microsoft Word, for instance, has features for highlighting spelling and grammatical errors – the usual squiggly line under the words it feels are out of context or misspelt, or the in-built dictionary which can be adjusted for different languages and variations in style, e.g. American English versus British English – and none of these is considered cheating. But realistically, AI is doing the work for you. And the usage is growing. As Hutson et al. (2022, p. 3953) note, 'Even as we write this article, AI is providing suggestions on how to finish sentences and recommending changes.' And whilst you cannot use writing that has been constructed by AI (albeit, I would say 'watch this space'), there are a growing number of uses for its official inclusion. For example, some institutions state that despite the premise that writing should be your own construction, the initial framework or structure may have been devised using AI.

Moreover, there are many useful tools for reading and summarising articles – ChatGPT, for instance – that can help you to identify themes within your literature, and some of these may be considered acceptable. If you do decide to use these, however, you should bear in mind that they are never a substitution for actual reading. Where possible, you should always engage on a personal level with academic texts. Otherwise, you commit a huge disservice to yourself as a scholar. If an AI program is interpreting your article and providing all your references, what have you really gained from the experience? Undertaking a degree is about self-development and intellectual growth, and this can only (presently) be achieved through personal engagement with resources. Whatever you choose to use, then, you should ensure that you are still developing your study skills and growing personally as a scholar of your field. And, of course, you may need to acknowledge the process you have undertaken by citing the particular AI program.

We do not know the future of AI in universities, but we can predict that there is going to be a significant impact in some way. Indeed, some of this is already under way (Bearman et al., 2022). What I would argue, however, is that using AI too heavily denies you of the skill acquisition that you so rightly deserve from your HE study; namely, the criticality, the engagement with the academic literature, the cognitive grappling with theory and practice, the intellectual underpinning needed to analyse concepts, strategies and arguments, and, of course, the in-class debates. This is the development of the mind at its best and is an essential component of higher education. Without it, we merely become computer programme operators. If that is your career goal – so, be it! But it should not define your role in HE.

▶ WHAT ARE YOUR FEARS?

A good exercise for you to do in the early period of your studies is perhaps to deal with your gremlins. We all have them and some are more powerful than others. However, some of your fears as a mature student are likely to be the same fears as your younger peers, and probably even the same as anyone facing something different, such as starting a new job. Here is a list (you may have more) of some of the common fears and feelings that people have when delving into the unknown:

- Low self-esteem
- Confidence concerns
- Lack of experience
- Feeling out of the habit
- Perceived inability
- Impostor syndrome
- Problems with time management and organisation skills
- Poor motivation
- Belief that you are on the wrong course
- Financial worries
- Familial commitments

Strategies for addressing some of these will be discussed as you progress through the book, but it is important to reassure yourself that these are all typical concerns or challenges for mature people returning to education. And whilst some are more difficult than others, they are all areas that you can address in some way or for which there is a wealth of support available. Confidence, for instance, is a major concern for many mature students but it often does not reflect ability. That is, mature students are more likely to be lacking in confidence even though they are perfectly capable (and in many cases more than capable) of competing with their peers. In a review of the literature on mature students in higher education, Richardson (1994) challenged the notion that mature students were lacking in the necessary fundamental skills required for succeeding in their studies. Instead, he suggested that they were more likely to engage in deep and meaningful approaches to learning. Often, the experiences of mature students provide a solid foundation for independent study.

▶ WAITING TO BEGIN YOUR STUDIES

With such a significant transition ahead of you, you will likely have a lot of questions that need answering, and having to wait several months to start your course can be angst-inducing. A good institution will recognise this and thus remain in contact with their future students as a way of alleviating any anxiety. Many HEIs offer 'keeping warm' sessions or some form of preparation event to maintain and build on the initial connection they have with you. This works well in most cases, particularly where students may have had prior concerns regarding their choice of institution or their level of academic preparedness. It builds a strong relationship between the individual and the HEI and enables you as a future student to feel valued. After all, if Institution A has not bothered to drop you an email after 6 months to at least say 'hi, we haven't forgotten you' or 'here is what you could be doing in the meantime,' yet Institution B has been with you every step of the way – providing you with reading lists, websites, information on key people in the field, and regular updates on what to expect – it is not difficult to see where your loyalties may lie. Feeling valued is important and we all need it. If you are in a situation where Institution A is your main choice, then, you could perhaps consider contacting them (or going with your second option). Good universities recognise that the students are more likely to be retained if they feel that they belong (Thomas, 2012). And students who feel they belong are much more likely to see their studies through to the end. In addition, you may wish to link up with future students through a Facebook or WhatsApp group. This can allay many fears of the unknown you might have. Linking with like-minded individuals also prevents many of those uncomfortable moments when you first arrive on the campus and meet your fellow students.

> **Box 1.1   Activity**
>
> Identify the range of effective support mechanisms that are in place in the university of your choice. These might be money-related, focused on mental health advice and counselling, or they could be centred on study skills. If you have not yet chosen somewhere, check out the website of a possible option to see what it offers.

▶ LEARNING AS A HABIT

Successful study often arises from the formation of habits, routines, or regular behaviours that you incorporate into your life. If it has been some time since you last engaged in formal learning, you may feel that you have a lot of ground to cover to catch up. In order to become a successful student, you should have a focus for your study (your goals, for instance) and position studying as an essential component of your weekly routine (see also Chapter 3). This does not mean that studying is easy, of course. But forming a habit means that you can condition yourself to challenge some of the initial obstacles you face, such as the previously mentioned low confidence. When you are out of the routine of learning, it is perfectly natural to feel that you are somehow incapable of resurrecting it. Habit-forming is useful and productive because it speaks volumes to our mindset and challenges negative thoughts. It is our way of telling ourselves that it is just something we do.

Incorporating study as a regular part of your weekly routine is essential as it reaffirms this positive message and helps you to focus. As an example, you may feel that riding a bike is easy but that would be because you have already mastered it. However, think about how daunting that prospect was the first time you sat on the bike. How difficult was it to take your feet off the floor, for instance? What you needed to do was to overcome that obstacle, and one effective way to do this was to practise, numerous times, moving the pedals forward whilst sustaining your balance.

Such repetition, particularly if performed in the same way each time, can lead to a temporary habit (and, eventually, a new activity). Getting on the bike every day for a week, for instance, not only helps you to overcome the fear of the unknown, it also becomes a naturalised activity – i.e. just something that you now do. And each day your confidence grows (providing you do not fall off) as you become familiar and more comfortable with the activity. Even the manner in which you conceptualise the process will change, e.g. 'I can't ride a bike' becomes 'I need to ride my bike more proficiently.' And eventually, of course, you state, 'I can ride a bike.' Habit forming, then, can help us to break through the fear of inability. Of course, this does not mean that you will not feel challenged at times. But forming your habit, and therefore taking small steps, will enable you to progress more efficiently and ultimately achieve your goal. In a similar manner, you should realise that the ability to develop academically is achievable, albeit with a little hard work and commitment. Studying is far more rewarding when you make the effort, and for fun let's draw on Newton's Third Law for inspiration: 'for every action there is an equal and opposite reaction.' That is, you get out of it what you put in.

In the next chapter we will look at some of the skills needed for successful study in HE and discuss how these can also be developed as you progress.

▶ REFERENCES

Bearman, M., Ryan, J., & Ajjawi, R. (2022). Discourses of artificial intelligence in higher education: A critical literature review. *Higher Education, 86*. https://doi.org/10.1007/s10734-022-00937-2

Britton, J., Dearden, L., van der Erve, L., & Waltmann, B. (2020). *The impact of undergraduate degrees on lifetime earnings* (pp. 1–86). Institute for Fiscal Studies. https://doi.org/10.1920/re.ifs.2020.0167

Bureau of Labor Statistics. (2023). *News release: Number of jobs, labor market experience, marital status, and health for those born 1957–1964*. Bureau of Labor. https://www.bls.gov/news.release/pdf/nlsoy.pdf

Christensen, G., Steinmetz, A., Alcorn, B., Bennett, A., Woods, D. and Emanuel, E.J. (2013). The MOOC phenomenon: Who takes massive open online courses and why? *SSRN Electronic Journal*. https://doi.org/10.2139/ssrn.2350964

Cremin, L. A. (1976). *Public education*. Basic Books.

Dewey, J. (1997). *Experience and education*. Free Press.

Hilgard, E. R., Kimble, G. A., & Marquis, D. G. (1961). *Hilgard and Marquis' conditioning and learning*. Appleton Century.

Hubble, S., & Bolton, P. (2021). *Mature higher education students in England*. https://researchbriefings.files.parliament.uk/documents/CBP-8809/CBP-8809.pdf

Hutson, J., Jeevanjee, T., Graaf, V. V., Lively, J., Weber, J., Weir, G., Arnone, K., Carnes, G., Vosevich, K., Plate, D., Leary, M., & Edele, S. (2022). Artificial intelligence and the disruption of higher education: Strategies for integrations across disciplines. *Creative Education*, *13*(12), 3953–3980. https://doi.org/10.4236/ce.2022.1312253

Kirschner, P. A., Sweller, J., & Clark, R. E. (2006). Why minimal guidance during instruction does not work: An analysis of the failure of constructivist, discovery, problem-based, experiential, and inquiry-based teaching. *Educational Psychologist*, *41*(2), 75–86. https://doi.org/10.1207/s15326985ep4102_1

Matsouka, K., & Mihail, D. M. (2016). Graduates' employability. *Industry and Higher Education*, *30*(5), 321–326. https://doi.org/10.1177/0950422216663719

Office for National Statistics. (2022). *Job changers and stayers, understanding earnings, UK: April 2012 to April 2021*. Office for National Statistics. www.ons.gov.uk. https://www.ons.gov.uk/employmentandlabourmarket/peopleinwork/earningsandworkinghours/articles/jobchangersandstayersunderstandingearningsukapril2012toapril2021/april2012toapril2021#overview

Office for Students. (2021). OfS Insight 9. Improving opportunity and choice for mature students. In *www.officeforstudents.org* (pp. 1–11). Office for Students. https://www.officeforstudents.org.uk/media/19b24842-52a0-41d1-9be2-3286339f8fde/ofs-insight-brief-9-updated-10-may-2022.pdf

Office for Students. (2023, December 18). *A statistical overview of higher education in England – Office for Students*. www.officeforstudents.org.uk. https://www.officeforstudents.org.uk/publications/annual-review-2023/a-statistical-overview-of-higher-education-in-england/#_edn79

Pearce, N. (2017). Exploring the learning experiences of older mature undergraduate students. *Widening Participation and Lifelong Learning*, *19*(1), 59–76. https://doi.org/10.5456/wpll.19.1.59

Richardson, J.T.E. (1994). Mature students in higher education: I. A literature survey on approaches to studying. *Studies in Higher Education*, *19*(3), (pp. 309–325). https://doi.org/10.1080/03075079412331381900.

Thomas, L. (2012). *Building student engagement and belonging in Higher Education at a time of change: Final report from the What Works? Student Retention & Success programme final report* (pp. 1–102). Paul Hamlyn Foundation. https://s3.eu-west-2.amazonaws.com/assets.creode.advancehe-document-manager/documents/hea/private/what_works_final_report_1568036657.pdf

▶ USEFUL WEBSITES

https://www.khanacademy.org/
https://www.mooc.org/

2 Developing Your Study Skills

▶ INTRODUCTION

Everything you do in your university studies is linked in some way. Whilst some links may seem tenuous, others will be more explicit, and identifying connections will enable you to see the bigger picture. If you finish one module and start the next, for instance, think about how they are connected. How do they relate to each other? What have you already learned that you can take forward? How does your independent study complement the process? Questions such as these help you to develop an overview of your learning journey. If you are serious about making your studies work for you and your goals, it is useful to see how everything is connected and how everything has potential to benefit you in your chosen career. This means viewing everything through the lens of you as a future professional working in this area. Fast-forward five years, for example, and ask yourself how this could be of use to you? Of course, learning is not just about the end point of securing a career. But whether your passion is career-focused or purely for the love of the subject, there are many benefits to understanding the wider relevance of what you are doing.

DOI: 10.4324/9781032619255-2

In this way, you can enjoy all the elements of your learning journey and thus maximise the benefits personally.

Part of the enjoyment of undertaking a degree is seeing how you grow as an individual scholar, and there are many ways to contribute to your learning journey that go beyond merely attending sessions and writing up your assignments. Contributing in class, for instance, can be fun and interesting and it helps to consolidate your knowledge. All students have a role to play in their university learning and participation improves the overall experience for everyone. Engagement is also an essential part of your journey as you are aiming to become an independent and autonomous learner. And this sets you up to achieve success in your career as well, because it is about who you are as both a scholar of your field and a future professional.

▶ FINDING YOUR STUDY SPACE

University libraries were once places that held incredible collections of informative reference materials and educational resources – e.g. journals, books, magazines, specialist artworks, microfilms, educational DVDs, CDs, and so on – that could be used for research or other scholarly engagement. Students and academics would visit in person, spending hours each day traversing through a wealth of resources as they engaged in some of the desk-based research or background reading. But libraries are no longer mere 'codex curators' (Desmarchelier et al., 2024, p. 1). Instead, access to resources is now encouraged via virtual exploration, and many libraries are rebranding as social learning spaces where students network and discuss ideas and assignments over coffee. This is perhaps moving with the times – we now have instant access to the latest articles at any hour of the day and technology is at our fingertips. But there is also growing academic anxiety in the modern world, where funding is competitive and institutions are subject to precarity. As such, 'technology has come to represent a mechanism being used to dismantle the modern university' (Earhart, 2018, p. 394). In support of this, Elmborg (2011, p. 338) claims that 'Libraries, with their historical ethos of free access for all, struggle to justify their existence in a world of 24/7 access increasingly evaluated by profit-based, commercial metrics.'

Despite this, there are lots of study benefits to take from a shift to greater online access. For instance, most of the resources you need for your assignment will be available to you on your home computer or laptop, and you no longer need to visit the library in person. This means that you can work in the comfort of your own home, taking breaks when necessary and not worrying about the long walk home in the rain. You could also give in to that urge to get out of bed at 3am (if that's where the mood takes you) to jot down those insomnia-inducing ideas that have plagued you for the last few hours and catch up on your reading. With online access to journals and ebooks 24 hours per day, then, you can undertake your studying whenever it suits. (But this might also mean that there are no excuses for a late submission – sorry!)

Despite the luxury of working online, there are also many benefits in physically attending the library. Some excel in sharing a learning space with like-minded individuals (Bourdieu, 1979), feeling safe and comfortable knowing that their peers are also engaged in studying. And the library is usually a quiet place to study and might be more conducive to learning than studying at home, particularly as home is the same environment in which you do all your cooking, cleaning, showering and relaxing. Furthermore, not only does physically visiting a place help you to differentiate between your studying time and home life, it also places temporal parameters on it, i.e. you work a set number of hours before leaving the library and finishing for the day. This helps you to really switch off when needed. However, if you have a preference for studying at home, and are motivated, have strong time management and organisational skills (see Chapter 3), and are determined to make it work, there are some points you should consider in order to ensure it will be effective.

Studying at home

It is useful when studying at home to have an area in which you can work. Create a learning space that you can use for studying but also one that you can move away from to demonstrate closure. You do not always need the luxury of having a home study, however. Even an area in the kitchen – perhaps sat at a dining table – or in a bedroom can work, so long as you can make a distinction at some point. This might mean setting up your laptop and your books and arranging the area to signify a study space. As long as this is your quiet area, exempt from distractions, and that you are comfortable in it, it can be as productive as anywhere else. What is perhaps important, however, is restoring that space once you finish. The table without books, laptop, learning aids, and maybe even your iPhone playing Classic FM (a step too far?) becomes a dining table once again and you distinguish between your home life and your university studies. Thus, the bespoke space encourages you to maintain a strong balance between your studies and your home life.

It is also useful to avoid having thoughts about your studying in your leisure periods as this prevents you from relaxing. Whilst learning does not happen in a vacuum – it is not something that is confine to the classroom, for instance – and thought processes at any time can be essential for forming meaning from your experiences, there does need to be a point at which you can switch off from one activity and switch on to another. Categorising your time in this manner can help you to declutter your brain and enable you to focus on the task in hand. It is not easy to undertake but it can be developed over time if you practise.

Your learning space, then, is critical in helping you to situate your studying within the rest of the everyday activities in your life. Unless you have the privilege of having a personal study, set it up your space when you need it, use it, and then restore it to its former role when you finish. This gives your learning closure and is good for your mental health. And for those good at maths, you should be able to identify the proportion of your week that can be allocated for both studying and other activities you spend your time on. This is often a productive investment that yields many rewards, and a detailed example of how you can do this is given in the section entitled 'Juggling your commitments' in Chapter 4.

▶ STUDY BREAKS

A key ingredient in success, just as it is in leading a happy life, is balance. As the proverb goes, 'All work and no play makes Jack a dull [and arguably tired and unmotivated] boy.' Achieving success is not easy and often requires hard work. And even then, a little serendipity would not go amiss. But for work to be productive, it has to have a clear focus and be meaningful for you. And to create the balance needed for your hard efforts to pay off, you should reward yourself on occasions. For instance, you have been reading each week for over a month now and you have been taking notes on your reading, synthesizing the information, and trying to form new connections. You have done some writing each week as well in order to streamline your thoughts. And the culmination of all this work can be seen in today's efforts where you have finally submitted that assignment. Congratulations! That is a great achievement. And whilst you have not finished yet, you should take some time out to restore the balance. If possible, give yourself a little reward: take a couple of days off, go down to the coast or the beach, spend time with your loved ones and so on. This leisure time, informally known as 'zenning,' I believe, is very important for you to sustain your motivation.

Continuously working can result in burnout and this severely impacts on your energy levels and commitment. You obviously want to stay fresh and continue with your studies so it is important that you can return to them with energy and enthusiasm. Study breaks allow your body to return to normal after long periods of intensity. When you take a break, therefore, you might want to consider exercising for added benefits of reducing your stress levels and addressing your apathy and lack of motivation. As Mikkelsen et al., 2017, p. 49) notes, a 'depressed mood, which is associated with increased anger, confusion, fatigue, tension, and reduced vigour, could be alleviated by exercise.' In addition, exercise also helps to alleviate stress as it prompts the production of endorphins, those well-known feel-good hormones in the brain (Amir et al., 1980; Ali et al., 2021).

Study breaks provide you with the impetus to resume your quest because they send out the hugely important message that 'this intense working is temporary and will soon end.' A significant part of the stress that emanates from someone's job or home life is the thought that there is no way out and that this may never end, at least not in a nice way. So, it is important to retain that message and to tell yourself that studying does have its difficult parts, it can be intense, but the balance is good and will not affect us in a detrimental way so long as we know when to take on extra workloads and when (and how) to rest and recuperate. To achieve this balance, you may be interested in a structured approach to your studying, such as the Pomodoro technique.

The Pomodoro technique

This is discussed a lot in self-help books and offers a systematic approach to taking breaks. The research into this is still underexplored but it does appear to have some lasting benefits over the setting of your own breaks (See Biwer et al., 2023). The structure works for many people as it allows them to concentrate on what is important (studying), and it removes that added pressure of regularly thinking about when an appropriate time to factor in a break might be. Stopping for a break merely when you remember is not a healthy approach. You might keep stopping and get very distracted. Or you might push yourself too much which becomes counterproductive after a while. Moreover, keeping an 'I must remember to stop at some point' message on your mind is arguably draining for your cognitive processing capacity and it can serve as a significant distraction, such as 'clock watching.' The easiest way to do this, then, is to set up a timer, such as the one you have on your phone. Set it to 25 minutes and then switch your concentration onto your work. Of course, you might need to prepare beforehand so the study session might look a little something like this:

> Make your favourite drink (water is good either as well or instead), gather any necessities, such as healthy snacks, and identify your study space. Let's suppose you have a desk with your computer or laptop on and can arrange some of your books alongside. (Online resources are obviously fine as well.) Switch the computer on and call up the folder with the assignment documents in. This might include your draft on a Word document and perhaps some articles you have saved or noted, depending on the aim of the session.

Once you have everything you need you are ready to start so hit that timer button and set the phone aside. You should now concentrate on the task in hand and try not to become distracted. If you have thoughts of other things, aim to push them out your head until after the 25 minutes. You might even be able to prepare for this if you know the sorts of thoughts you are likely to get – e.g. the washing up needs doing before you go to bed or the cat needs feeding. If you cannot do your tasks before you start, record them on a to-do list so you can forget about them temporarily.

When the timer is activated, stop, reset it to five minutes and then take a break. It is not essential what you do here so long as you are not focused on your work. Ideally, you will move away from the computer, stretch your legs, and do something significantly different (perhaps now is the time to give Squiggles his dinner). After five minutes, your alarm will activate again. Reset it and resume your studies, repeating the 25-minute process.

Hopefully you will find from this that the structure encourages you to engage with the task and that you enjoy the time in between. If you need to look at your phone or check your social media, do it in the five-minute break. But be strict with yourself and stick to the timing, otherwise you are not really in a position to take maximum benefit from it. You can then evaluate the process to see if it works for you. Is it something that you will continue with? When you do this, however, you must give it a fair chance by sticking to the timings and the general conduct outlined above. If after you have tried the 25–5 method you find that it still does not work for you, perhaps you need to set your own breaks. Personally, I like to work in stints of an hour or two and then take slightly longer breaks, in which I reward myself with something I like to do. I may even use the time to catch up on other demands, such as personal organisation or even tidying up (I don't have a cat, sorry). What matters is that this time is guilt-free and that I can refocus and return to my work, knowing that other items that were on my mind – that clock still needs a battery or the children's toys still need to be put away, for example – can temporarily be discarded.

▶ PERFORMING UNDER TIMED CONDITIONS

If you suffer from anxiety or any other mental-health related condition, speak to your personal tutor as soon as you know that there will be exams involved. Your tutor will help you to prepare and may even signpost you to further help. Exam conditions can be stressful, but you can prepare for an exam in a similar way to preparing your assignment (see Chapter 3), giving yourself a schedule to follow for your revision and ensuring that your notes are meaningful and can be translated into a written response. You might even find that the Pomodoro technique helps you to compartmentalise your time and be strict with yourself. Working in an exam just means that you are timed in what you produce. This is an opportunity for you to demonstrate what you can do, however, and one positive outcome from the timing means that once you finish you can forget about it for the rest of the day. As such, you can make the structure work in your favour. As with your assignments, though, you need to identify a structure for your response. If it is a written exam, think about what you will say and how you will say it. Then, identify your structure so that the writing will flow coherently and sequentially, i.e. the argument builds or there is evidence of why you have moved from one point to another. Even a simple structure like the one below can work well:

❖ Introduction
❖ Point 1
❖ Point 2
❖ Point 3
❖ Point 4
❖ Discussion
❖ Conclusion

This is basic but effective and you can adapt it to suit your needs. Let's assume you need to write an essay on whether plastic drinking vessels should replace glass ones in the leisure industry. The way you structure it might be something like this:

❖ Introduction
❖ The leisure industry
❖ The dangers associated with glass
❖ Cost implications
❖ Plastic and the environment
❖ Discussion
❖ Conclusion

Maybe you even decide that you need another point or perhaps some context after the introduction? Or you might wish to include a section that outlines the studies you have read and their significance (similar to a literature review). You can allocate both time and, if you feel you need it, a word count to each section. Time is better, however, because counting words is time consuming and unnecessary (particularly as exams are usually handwritten). You may, however, have a visual understanding of the writing – that is, you can see by looking at each section if you think it is long enough. More importantly, of course, is that the content, timings and word counts should only serve as loose guides. You should aim to be succinct, include the relevant points, and avoid verbiage (which amounts to waffle). The strength of timing each section (or the response as a whole) is that you do not run out of time.

Here is an example of what you might have from a computer science exam:

Duration: Three hours
Sections to complete: Five (one question from each; however, each section also contains sub-questions)
Marks per section: 20

The sections are equally weighted in that you can score up to 20 points for each. However, the length of the sub-questions varies, some offering two marks and others offering 8. You can engage in this level of granularity if you wish, but a much more straightforward process would be to allocate time for each section. A simple maths calculation tells us that you need to spend around a fifth of your time on each section. If you write for two hours and you are still on section one, then you are not using your time wisely. You can only score a maximum of 20 points for that section, regardless of how well-detailed your response is.

In the example, three hours does not equally divide into five. A good rule of thumb, then, would be to spend around 30 minutes on each section. This leaves you some time at the end to read over your responses and perhaps return to those weaker sections to develop them. Spreading your time in this way is essential as it enables you to maximise your chances for achieving your best score. It is also how this exam paper is created. If the sections had unequal grading values, where the marks varied for each, you would have to devote different amounts of time for each. If you find yourself in an exam where this appears to be the case, you should conduct your calculation accordingly. For instance, if section two on the example was worth 40 points but sections three and four were only worth 10, we could simply adapt the time thus:

Section 1 – 30 mins
Section 2 – 60 mins
Section 3 – 15 mins
Section 4 – 15 mins
Section 5 – 30 mins

It may seem daunting looking at this, but it is really a simple calculation and worth spending a minute or two at the start so that you can adhere to your structure. Another way to look at this exam could be to allocate 1.5 minutes per point (1.5 x the number of points). This is the granularity mentioned earlier. So, a 6-point question would require around nine minutes to answer, and an 8-point question would be allocated twelve minutes. The marks allocated for the questions, then, tell us how much time, comparatively, we should spend on each. If the idea of doing calculations at the beginning is stressful and merely adding to your exam anxiety, try to keep your approach as simple as possible. This is designed to help you make the most of the exam rather than unnecessarily distract you so you may have to adapt it to suit your needs. Where possible, practising with previous exam papers can help you to overcome your fears.

▶ FILE MANAGEMENT

Now that you have identified how and when you like to study, and have some strategies for approaching your assessments, it is necessary for you to think about how and where you will store your work. To do this, let's utilise the concept introduced early in this chapter of 'seeing the bigger picture' of your learning journey and fulfilling your goal of becoming a knowledgeable and experienced professional in the field. In this way, your learning is never wasted and you can keep track of your progress. You should structure your files, then, so they can be of use to you throughout your degree (and possibly beyond). For example, you are undertaking a module later in your studies and a familiar theme arises. You then recall that you once conducted a literature review on this topic and realise that this is of use to you now. Fortunately, you structured your files well and it is easy to locate. You revisit the review and it signposts you to some useful readings and highlight points that you now wish to explore in more detail. To be clear, this is not advocating plagiarism as you are not looking to recycle your words; rather, it acts a foundation for further enquiry. And of course this is exactly what a degree should do – provide a foundation from which you can build and develop this as you progress.

Thinking ahead, then, you should arrange your files so that they are meaningful. If you are disorganised, you might find yourself saving your work in a variety of places, often unrelated, so it is beneficial for you to take control of this from the outset. Here is an example of poor practice from this academic year (at the time of writing) from a student called John (pseudonym):

> In the induction week, John saved stuff onto the desktop on a university computer for convenience, with a view to moving it a later date (**NB**. Novice error – very rarely do people get round to doing this). In the second week he was reminded of the university's cloud and saved some other files on that. In the evenings, however, he was storing files on his hard drive at home. On one occasion in class he stated, 'Two nights ago I was at my sister's house and was using her laptop. I didn't have a USB with me so I saved my assignment in her 'My Documents' area. John lost some of his work (or at least could not locate it again) and this impacted on his grade for his first assignment. He submitted late as a result of redoing several sections of his assignment and this was capped at pass. John is a bright and otherwise very capable student and after this episode he never scored lower than a 2i in his assignments.

Fortunately, with a little help, John is now much more organised and in control of his work. But this is not an unrealistic picture of how many of us function at times, particularly if we haven't thought something through in any depth. If you fail to establish good practice from the outset, this can leave you many difficulties to deal with later on. It is worth investing some time, then, so let's have a look at some strategies. Firstly, a file for each module you are studying is perhaps a necessity. Then, subfolders relating to assignments or key activities might work well. However, you should avoid having subfolders in subfolders in subfolders...and so on. This represents 'mind clutter'. If possible, have your main folder (parent) for the module and a series of subfolders (child folders) within that. Using the 'parent' and 'child' language is useful and ideally you only have one parent but many children. You can have numerous children but no grandchildren as your

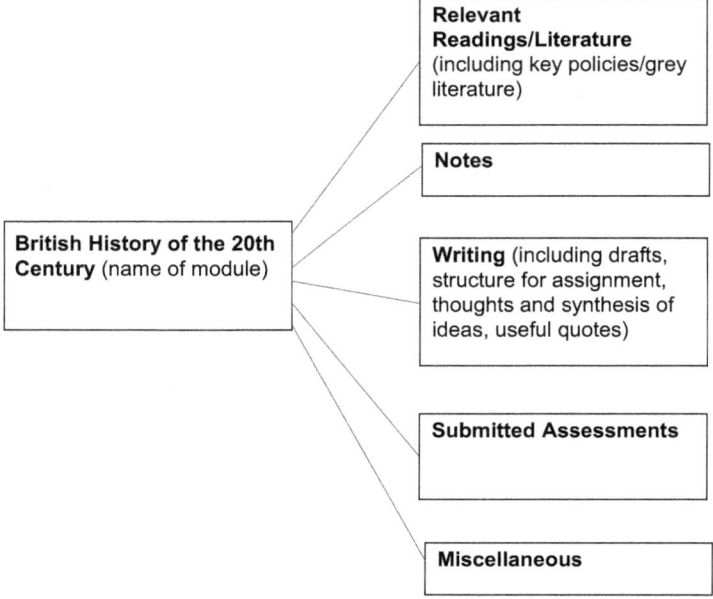

Figure 2.1 File Management.

children are too young. This results in a much more manageable system. One of the child folders should probably be for 'miscellaneous' items so that you can save all your seemingly unrelated items together. This is good for anything that you are not sure of and means that you don't need to stress yourself with thinking up names for folders that have duplicate contents or may never be of use.

The figure is an example of a useful filing system for a first-year student of a BA in History (Figure 2.1).

▶ BACKING UP YOUR WORK

Regardless of whatever cloud or impeccable storage device you save your work on, you should always consider backing it up further. No system is infallible so it is always worth having that safety net. Even if you never need it, what harm has it done? It doesn't take long to back up your work and you should do it on a regular basis, depending on how much you have added to it. If you are in the process of writing up your assignment, it is a good strategy to back it up after each session. A day may not seem much, but it can make a significant difference when you lose 2,000 words and realise that all your hard work has been wasted. Ideally, back up your work on another device, such as a USB or another computer. Using the cloud is great but, as already stated, nothing is infallible and even though that international threat of a cyber-attack might sound like science fiction, do you really want to risk losing everything?

When you are backing up your work, make sure that you label it correctly. This is a back-up copy and it can be confusing if you have multiple copies of the same file, particularly when you work across devices. You might have your home PC, for instance, and, like John, have saved files on the university drives. This is fine but do you know for sure which one is the master version? Many people also have several versions of their document, particularly if they are sharing it with peers, such as PowerPoint slides for a group presentation. These are often labelled as 'Latest' or 'New' and then emailed around. But these are meaningless labels and will inevitably cause you problems. Which 'latest' is the latest, for instance? Who had it last? What happens to the 'New' document when you edit it? Is the old one now the new one, etc? Even dating the document can be confusing unless you know the exact time the latest version was edited. Fortunately, this is easily solved with a shared drive that saves one file only. All the group can access it and all changes are saved, even for the most part if two or more people are editing it simultaneously.

For your own work and using multiple devices, however, it can be frustrating to work on an assignment on one device and then forget and start typing on another. This is easily achieved, even when you are being careful, so think wisely about where you should save and access your work. Dedicate a base for your work – e.g. 'I only save the master file on my laptop at home. All others are duplicates in the event of my laptop crashing' – and identify where the back-ups will sit. Finally, label your back-up folder appropriately.

Something like 'Copy of master folder' might help you to keep track of duplicates. In the next chapter we will look a little deeper into organisational skills and explore how getting to grips with your time management will facilitate an effective approach to your learning.

▶ REFERENCES

Ali, A. H., Ahmed, H. S., Jawad, A. S., & Mustafa, M. A. (2021). Endorphin: Function and mechanism of action. *Science Archives, 02*(01), 09–13. https://doi.org/10.47587/sa.2021.2102

Amir, S., Brown, Z. W., & Amit, Z. (1980). The role of endorphins in stress: Evidence and speculations. *Neuroscience and Biobehavioral Reviews, 4*(1), 77–86. https://doi.org/10.1016/0149-7634(80)90027-5

Biwer, F., Wiradhany, W., Oude Egbrink, M.G.A. & de Bruin, A.B.H. (2023). Understanding effort regulation: Comparing 'Pomodoro' breaks and self-regulated breaks. *British Journal of Educational Psychology*, [online] *93*(S2). https://doi.org/10.1111/bjep.12593

Bourdieu, P. (1979). *Distinction: A social critique of the judgement of taste*. Routledge.

Desmarchelier, B., Djellal, F., & Gallouj, F. (2024). Public libraries as social innovators. *Public Library Quarterly*, 1–20. https://doi.org/10.1080/01616846.2024.2357399

Earhart, A. E. (2018). The book in the age of academic anxiety. *American Literary History, 30*(2), 394–401. https://www.jstor.org/stable/48546521

Elmborg, J. K. (2011). Libraries as the spaces between us: Recognizing and valuing the third space. *Reference & User Services Quarterly, 50*(4), 338–350. https://www.jstor.org/stable/20865425

Mikkelsen, K., Stojanovska, L., Polenakovic, M., Bosevski, M., & Apostolopoulos, V. (2017). Exercise and mental health. *Maturitas, 106*(106), 48–56. https://doi.org/10.1016/j.maturitas.2017.09.003

3 Time Management and Organisational Skills

▶ **INTRODUCTION**

Time management and organisational skills are not traits that come naturally to us as humans. Whilst we crave routine and rely on self-governance, these skills are often in need of development. And it is usually those of us who have experience of managing their own time and demonstrating an ability to organise themselves effectively who appear to be naturally gifted and successful. But these skills have to be developed and honed through experience and as such require an investment in planning and self-analysis. Such an investment can pay significant dividends in the long run, and as a mature student wishing to glean the maximum benefit from learning it is certainly worthwhile spending the time to establish a foundation upon which you can grow and develop in the most efficacious manner. Successful study is within your grasp and this chapter will hopefully enable you to take control of your learning journey.

DOI: 10.4324/9781032619255-3

Juggling your commitments

As a mature student, you are likely to have a lot of competing events in your life, such as living expenses – a mortgage or rental agreement, household bills, weekly shopping and so on – or perhaps children or other familial commitments that require you to divide up your time accordingly. This might seem difficult but putting in place some simple strategies can generate an effective and highly productive schedule for your working week. This includes the time it takes to work, sleep, study, spend time with your family, and engage in a little downtime for yourself. And it is not enough to merely identify sleep as your downtime, you will also need to factor in quiet periods for reflecting and refocussing. Ideally, this involves doing something you enjoy, preferably an activity that is not related to your study commitments. If spending time with your loved ones helps you to wind down then that is great, but it might be that you need an additional focus – perhaps a little 'you' time. This balance is essential for productivity and in order to get this right you may need to think a little mechanically, at least until you form your new routine. The timetable below, adapted from a book for FE teachers (Allan, 2022), can be used to map out your week. Of course, getting a grip on your hourly expenditure may sound like you are producing a profit and loss statement, but it can really help you to identify where the gaps are in your working week. And the principle is the same if you view time as potential capital – e.g. time in and time out signifies profit and loss.

Time in is easy, it doesn't change. You have a functioning week of 168 hours. You will need around six–nine hours per night of sleep (42–63 hours for sleep) and that leaves you with 105–126 hours. Suppose you have to work two days in a part-time job (around 18 hours including travel) and let's devote three generous hours per day for eating (21 hrs). You now have 66–87 hours. University lectures and travel may take around 10 for the week but let's say 15. This leaves you with 51–72 hours. Your expected study hours for a full-time course will need to be taken from the remainder. Some degrees will be more intensive, such as those with placements, and some will be more focused on the individual engagement and independent study. However, as it is easier to downsize a schedule than it is to grow it, let's assume that you will study for 35 hours per week. We have already allocated 15 hours for university lectures and other teaching sessions (again, due to variety across courses this is a ballpark figure). The other 20, then, will need to come from your 51–72. You now have 31–52 hours to engage in some downtime, perhaps some fun socialising with friends. Whilst this seems like a purely mechanical exercise, it is an effective way of understanding how your time is being spent and thus how you can plan to spend your time.

▶ CONSTRUCTING YOUR SCHEDULE

As early as possible in your studies you should work at establishing a routine that will pay off for you – a routine that will maximise your chances for success, will facilitate space for the tasks you need to undertake, and will reward you with time to spend on relaxing and what makes you feel happy and fulfilled. If you do not have a routine, you might be under considerably more stress and waste many hours reflecting on your aimlessness. For many in this situation, the cyclical process of non-productivity becomes the routine. If you know, therefore, that you will form a routine anyway, why not take control and devise your routine?

Table 3.1 provides an example of how you can construct your timetable, based on studying and other commitments, such as paid employment and leisurely pursuits.

The shaded areas represent your study time and as you can see it is a full timetable. In fact, it is an unusually heavy timetable, but this is deliberate because courses vary and it is arguably more useful to work from a busy one and adapt accordingly. Moreover, some full-time courses may require this many contact hours from you whilst others are much more focused on encouraging independent study, offering only around six hours of teaching per week.

TABLE 3.1 Example Weekly Timetable

Time and day	06:00 – 07:00	07:00 – 08:00	08:00 – 09:00	09:00 – 10:00	10:00 – 11:00	11:00 – 12:00	12:00 – 13:00	13:00 – 14:00	14:00 – 15:00	15:00 – 16:00	16:00 – 17:00	17:00 – 18:00	18:00 – 20:30
Mon	Shower and breakfast	Study time	Travel to uni Preparation time and socialising	Lecture	Seminar (break included)		Lunch	Teaching period (break included)			Travel home	Leisure time	Dinner Leisure time
Tues	Shower and breakfast	Study time	Study time				Lunch			Study time			Dinner Leisure time
Wed	Shower and breakfast	Study time	Travel to uni Preparation time and socialising	Lecture	Seminar (break included)		Lunch	Sports			Dinner Leisure time		
Thur	Shower and breakfast	Study time	Travel to uni Preparation time and socialising	Study time			Lunch	Teaching period (break included)			Travel home	Leisure time	Dinner Leisure time
Fri	Shower and breakfast	Study time	Travel to uni Preparation time and socialising	Teaching period (break included)			Lunch			Study time	Travel home	Leisure time	Dinner Leisure time
Sat	Shower and breakfast			Part-time work (including travel and breaks)								Dinner Leisure time	
Sun	Shower and breakfast			Part-time work (including travel and breaks)								Dinner Leisure time	

Even though the week on the timetable is a busy one, however, you will notice that all of your study occurs on a weekday. This frees up your weekend for employment and leisure time. Or, if you have the luxury of not needing to work at the weekends, it gives you more time to relax, network, engage in non-study-type activities and spend time with your family, thus generating a balance that is even more productive and rewarding for you. You may even use this flexibility to shuffle your hours round. Perhaps weekends are a good time for you to study, for instance, and you prefer a day off in the week. The main aspect to concentrate on is getting the balance right and making it right for you as a mature student. Study time is important, but you also have competing priorities and leisure time is essential to avoid burnout. Even with paid employment at the weekends, you should be able to switch off from studying and use the evenings to relax. But what about the times when you have an assignment due? If followed closely there is no need for extra study periods on those weekends. You can (and should) work on your assignment over a longer period of time. Whilst this means starting it earlier, you then benefit from only working on it during the allocated time frame of your balanced schedule. Your study periods are there for reading and writing (and thinking) and if you really make them work you could draft up your assignment – or at least a structure – with plenty of time before the deadline. During your preparation, then, your study periods are tailored to the focused reading and writing for your assignment. This takes the pressure off you and is well worth the investment as you can sustain a regular rhythm of study across the year, avoiding a 'manic one week, mellow the next' pattern of working.

Of course, there will be busy times during your degree as this can't always be avoided. If you are studying modules concurrently, for instance, it is likely that the assignments for each will be due around the same time. This can be difficult but thinking it through and using the planning time identified on your timetable should enable you to manage the situation well. For instance, how many hours do you need to set aside for Module A and how many for Module B? Are they both equal in weighting? Try to divide your time accordingly so that you do not focus intently on one to the detriment of the other. It is easy to neglect an assignment if you are embroiled in the writing of another one, so it is important to maintain the balance. If you have followed your timetable closely, it is unlikely that you will need to factor in any additional study time. Accepting that life is by no means straightforward, however, there may be busy times that you simply can't avoid. You can embrace these on a short-term basis, but you should aim to resume your regular pattern of working as soon as you can in order to minimise any detriment to your health and well-being.

The most important factor in all this, then, is balance. You are planning in such a detailed way because on the whole you want to make it work. But it can only work when the balance is right. Too much studying will lead to overload and burnout, and too little study will generate apathy. Both are clearly unwanted outcomes. In order to restore the balance, then, there are two caveats to consider when working extra hours:

1) You only allow the workload to encroach on your weekend or other leisure time on a short-term basis – this is <u>not</u> your new pattern.
2) You utilise the time after the mayhem to restore the balance. That is, if you have worked solidly over several weekends (on top of your working week) just to get that assignment in, you should then take a well-earned break.

The first instance avoids burnout as it is behaviour that is not sustained, whilst the second enables you to recover. Some students continually draw on the second instance, however, and it becomes their norm. That is, they do very little for many weeks but are then forced to put in lots of extra hours, including staying up all night on several occasions so they can catch up. And once they have submitted their work, they switch off again until the next 'rush' (around two weeks before the next deadline). If you do little else, promise yourself you will avoid this scenario as the long-term repercussions have little to no benefit whatsoever for you as a serious scholar.

For balance, you may also be able to take some time back during a reading week. Of course, your reading week should be just that

– an opportunity to catch up on or get ahead of your reading. But in the grand scheme of things, it is necessary to maintain your momentum through a happy medium. Balance is good for both your mind and your body, fuelling you to persevere during your studies in the healthiest way possible. A degree can be intense and often requires a huge commitment so you should avoid overloading yourself.

▶ MAKING IT WORK

In order to make your timetable work, you need to mimic the approach in the example yet tailor the study time to the course that you are on and the time you have available. This means factoring in your other commitments so that you have a clear and strong oversight of your working week. If you look at the example, you will see that the schedule is composed of heavy and light sessions. Tuesday, for instance, is a long and full-on day. However, it is offset by Wednesday afternoon, offering you time to switch off, engage with sports, and generally socialise with your peers. Traditionally, Wednesday afternoons are the periods where universities avoid running formal teaching sessions as it is the time when institutions compete against other on the astro turf, the rugby pitch, or in the basketball arena. That is, Wednesday afternoons are allocated for sports and students all over the UK use this time to compete with their student counterparts in other universities for a position in the sporting league tables (not to be confused with the official University Rankings). These are great opportunities for networking and enjoying yourself but do remember to incorporate them into your timetable.

As mentioned, it is likely that your own timetable will not have as many taught sessions or periods where you are required to attend. And Having fewer teaching sessions means that you can study comfortably in the manner of your choosing. However, this means that you have to be self-motivated. At this level, you cannot rely on your lecturers to tell you when to study. This is not school and there are many expectations when studying in HE, such as demonstrating a mature and productive approach. If you have fewer teaching periods you should make up the difference with independent study.

Should I stop the flow?

You may need to keep revising your timetable until you are happy that it can work for you. Ask yourself whether it can be realistically operationalised or whether it needs to be amended further. If you follow your timetable closely, there is no reason why it should hold you back. Once it has been established, therefore, you should adhere to it as much as you can to ensure you get the maximum rewards from it. For example, engage in the study periods and stop when each particular time period is over so that you can make the most of your leisure time. This balanced way of working can be extremely effective. Indeed, many professional writers allocate time to write and then immediately stop when that time ends, even if they are working productively and feel that they could carry on. They believe that regardless of their thought processes, their writing can be picked up again in the next session. This is a truly mechanistic manner of operating, but it works for those particular writers. Some even leave mid-sentence in order to adhere to their routine and justify this by stating it is easier to pick up an unfinished thought than it is to start a new one. What is clear from this, however, is the professional adherence to a schedule.

There are two schools of thought on this process of writing. One is that you should continue the productivity when writing as there may be lots of times when you find it hard to resume your writing due to the dreaded writer's block. If you have spent many hours in front of a blank screen and failed to write anything you will appreciate that when you do finally get motivated and start writing it can be frustrating to suddenly have to stop. But the alternative thinking on this, and the reason some professionals choose to stop when they do, is that you get to avoid burnout. Burnout is serious and it can happen really easily. It is a particular product of working in long and irregular cycles and thus represents an unbalanced and anti-routinised approach.

▶ FOLLOW YOUR GUT

If you have a study period and it does not work, don't be afraid to write the session off and start again the next day. It may be that you were tired and struggling to concentrate so doing even more work will not allow you to recover. Don't push that tiredness into your next study period; instead, subvert it. Stop, rest, resume! This is necessary for you to maximize your gains. After all, you may have been inactive in your last study period, but your brain was still active. And it will still perceive it as studying rather than leisure time.

Once you have established your routine, the more closely you can adhere to it the more effective your studying will be. Moreover, not only will it be easier for you to follow and therefore less mechanistic, you will get to know and learn your routine and thus accept it as a natural part of your week. You will no longer be trying to follow it but will in fact adhere to it much more closely as it becomes just what you do on that particular day. Moreover, your brain will thank you for the stability and uniform approach and you will no longer need to think deeply about what you are doing each day – save those profound deliberations for your theorising.

▶ LEISURE TIME

'Leisure time' is an overarching term used here to include all those activities that enable you to relax and unwind. After all, the highs are only highs because the lows exist. What that means is that you will be able to persevere during the more difficult periods because you know that you have other periods to enjoy. This is another reason why cramming and cycling your workload is not productive for you. When you cram, there is no respite; rather, you are working flat out until the highly pressured deadline arrives. This is not a healthy approach. Writing an assignment the night before the submission deadline does not buy you the luxury of stopping and saying, 'this is not working I will try again in half an hour or so.' Every moment needs to count when you cram because the pressure is on, and that in itself affects your productivity. It also impinges on your creativity and stops the ideas from flowing.

You may also have noticed that the leisure time on the timetable is at the end of the day, whilst there is a study period in the morning before you even start university. Supposing this was your timetable, you could swap the sessions around and resume your studying once you get home. That is your call, of course. But after a hard day you need to wind down, and you are likely to better perceive closure if that winding down coincides with the end of your working day and a physical move away from the university. In this way, you are not continuing your studying into the evening and moving it to a new environment. If you did insist on moving this period to later, it might be advisable for you to remain on campus for that hour and to travel back to your accommodation once you have finished. This still allows you clear closure and means that you compartmentalise your time more efficiently – studying takes place in the university, leisure time occurs at home. As such, you demarcate *study* and *relaxation* as two physical, as well as abstract, spaces.

▶ TERMLY PLANNING

In addition to your timetable, and arguably once you get it up and running, you may need to plan how your term, and possibly year, will look. Planning by term helps you to segment the year into more manageable time periods. You will have assignments to complete and other assessments throughout the term, and as mentioned earlier modules often run concurrently. Therefore, it is good to have an oversight of what is ahead of you. This helps you to shift your time around and it may be that you temporarily change your timetable for periods leading up to a significant deadline, i.e. you reallocate hours to work specifically on your assignment. Or perhaps an extra shift is available at your place of employment one weekend? Life often gets in the way, so it is necessary for you to adapt. Whilst the main purpose of planning is to give you a routine, it also enables you to meet any new demands head on. An example of a termly plan can be seen in Table 3.2.

TABLE 3.2 Example Termly Plan

SEPTEMBER

22 Terms starts *Attendance in uni (*first week students are in every day)	23 Attendance in uni	24 Attendance in uni	25 Attendance in uni	26 Attendance in uni	27 Module reading and in-class preparation	28 Module reading and in-class preparation
29 Module reading and in-class preparation	30 Work on group presentation					

OCTOBER

	1 Individual work on presentation	2 Work on group presentation	3 Module reading and in-class preparation	4 Work on group presentation	5 Module reading and in-class preparation
6 Reading for AB73 assignment	7 Reading for AB73 assignment	8 Reading for AB73 assignment	9 Work on group presentation	10 Draft of presentation	11 Leisure time – swimming	12 Extra study time (if needed)
13 Group presentation is ready	14 Reflections on group presentation	**15 Group presentation deadline**	16 Writing for AB73 assignment (plan and structure)	17 Writing for AB73 assignment (lit review)	18 Leisure time – walking	19 Extra study time (if needed)

(Continued)

TABLE 3.2 (CONTINUED) Example Termly Plan

20 Writing for AB73 assignment (policy context)	**21** Writing for AB73 assignment (discussion section)	**22** Writing for AB73 assignment (1st draft complete)	**23** Module readings	**24** Module readings	**25** Leisure time – swimming	**26** Extra study time (if needed)
27 Writing for AB73 assignment (revisions and editing of draft)	**28** Writing for AB73 assignment (revisions and editing of draft)	**29** AB73 assignment is ready	**30** Module readings. Submit AB73 assignment	**31 AB73 assignment due**		

NOVEMBER

					1 Leisure time	**2** Leisure time
3 Reading for AB74 assignment	**4** Reading for AB74 assignment	**5** Reading for AB74 assignment	**6** Reading for AB74 assignment	**7** Writing for AB74 assignment (plan and structure)	**8** Leisure time	**9** Leisure time
10 Reading for AB74 assignment	**11** Reading for AB74 assignment	**12** Writing for AB74 assignment (lit review)	**13** Writing for AB74 assignment (policy context)	**14** Writing for AB74 assignment (discussion section)	**15** Leisure time	**16** Leisure time
17 Writing for AB74 assignment (1st draft complete)	**18** Module readings	**19** Module readings	**20** Module readings	**21** Writing for AB74 assignment (revisions and editing of draft)	**22** Leisure time	**23** Leisure time

Time Management and Organisational Skills

24 Writing for AB74 assignment (revisions and editing of draft)	**25** Module readings	**26** Writing for AB74 assignment (revisions and editing of draft)	**27** Writing for AB74 assignment (revisions and editing of draft)	**28 AB74 assignment is ready**	**29** Leisure time	**30** Leisure time

DECEMBER

1 Module readings	**2** Module readings	**3 Submit AB74 assignment**	**4 AB74 assignment due**	**5** Leisure time	**6** Leisure time	**7** Leisure time
8 Preparation for next module	**9** Module readings	**10** Module readings	**11** Leisure time – reward yourself for all your hard work this term	**12 Term ends**		

You will notice from the example that preparation and writing-up time for your assignments has been incorporated. When you have a plan that is detailed in this way, deadlines should not be unexpected. They may seemingly come around quickly, but you should nevertheless be expecting each and every one of them and have planned accordingly. This means you will have completed the necessary work beforehand, including activities such as reading, drafting a plan, and/or preparing a presentation, as well as the more common undertakings such as actually writing your assignment. The preparation is an essential part of the process and should be considered within your termly plan. You might include two half days of focused reading, for instance, for one of your assignments.

You will also notice that the submission dates for each assignment are the day before the actual deadline. This (or earlier) is highly advisable. When you are trying to upload your assignment that is due in at 16:00 that day but it is now 15:58, and you are suddenly faced with an erratic, uncompromising and out of character drop box, you realise that technology is perhaps not your friend. As you watch that swirling icon in front of you, the tears welling in your eyes, you wonder where the time went and desperately wish that you could turn back the clock. This is not a stressful situation that you want to put yourself through, however. So be kind to yourself and get ahead of the game.

The detail of planning in this example is encroaching on the micro level and preparing it can be time consuming. But in the long run it can save you many hours of wasted effort and a lot of unnecessary thinking. On your plan, plot out your assignment deadlines first and then develop it from there. You can also colour-code it, perhaps making the weekends green to denote time for relaxation and activities of your choosing and highlighting the deadlines in red. In general, it is best to be thorough from the outset and include everything that you think is important as you can streamline it once you become more experienced in planning and have a better oversight of how your year will look. This exercise really is worth the investment, and even though you may not appreciate it at the beginning of term, you will see huge benefits as the academic year progresses. As with the weekly timetable discussed earlier, the purpose of this exercise is not to have you function robotically; rather, it is for you to take control of your learning and attain a detailed overview of your forthcoming milestones. Not only can this boost your confidence, it may enable you to achieve your academic goals for the year. And if done effectively, it will also give you a lot more time back.

▶ THE BENEFITS OF TIME MANAGEMENT

As part of your time management, you will need to decide how long you will allocate for producing your assessment. Let's say that you have an assignment to write that is 2,500 words long. In many ways the timeline is already there for you. You have a deadline and you are expected to submit on or before that date and time. But this will still need to be planned, especially if, as mentioned earlier, you are studying numerous modules concurrently. A good strategy is to start with your end date and work backwards. Let's say it is now the beginning of October and the deadline for your submission is December 15th. In order to feel comfortable, you would need to have a draft completed by around a week before, say the 8th, at the latest. If you allow a couple of weeks to write it, that takes us to 24th November. Also, what background work is needed before the writing begins? It is likely to be some reading of the literature and perhaps engaging with discussions in teaching sessions or through an online forum. You may even have to pitch an idea and present it many weeks before the assignment deadline. If you are also simultaneously working on other assignments, you will have to split your time accordingly. This might mean that you have on average a day a week to spend on this particular assignment. That is not very long and a day can pass very quickly if you are struggling to focus or do not know where to begin.

Chapters 7 and 8 will explore the writing process more closely so for now let's assume that a day per week will work. Suddenly, then, having four, five, and even six weeks to do an assignment is not a long time. You need to engage with the readings over a few weeks and allow your thoughts to develop. This process takes time because you need to make connections, synthesize theories, and formulate ideas. This is a constructive and creative process and requires a little more than skimming through an article and noting down a few quotes. In order to demonstrate criticality in your argument and in your writing, you will need to read with a critical eye (see Chapter 6). Engage with the ideas, challenge the arguments, and utilize a range of sources to ensure that the end result is robust. This means that one source is not enough. All studies are biased in some manner and all are flawed, however small or large that flaw may be. These flaws are known as limitations and are perfectly natural. So, reading around gives you a clearer and more comprehensive impression of the topic. It also shows you where there is conflict in the field and perhaps more research may be needed. As such, you can put the findings into context when you argue your points. But this all requires strong time management in order to achieve the maximum effect.

Hopefully, then, the exercises in this chapter demonstrate why the process of effective learning takes a little time, and why it is crucial to engage with a good study plan from the outset. You should also try to avoid seeing your assignments as tick-box exercises, or necessary evils you have to encounter in order to get that degree. Assessments are designed to enable you to consolidate your knowledge, and demonstrating this knowledge also informs your tutors of your progress on the module. But it is part of your learning journey. And planning it well, adhering to your timeframe, and taking time out to enjoy your subject will ensure that you are well on your way to achieving academic success. In the next chapter we will continue to explore the concept of taking control of your learning journey by discussing the roles of autonomy and independence when studying in higher education.

REFERENCE

Allan, D. (2022). *Developing resilience in FE teaching*. Abingdon, Oxon: Routledge.

4 Autonomy and Being an Independent Learner

▶ GROW YOUR AUTONOMY

As previously suggested in this book, you already have a wide range of skills to draw on as a mature student, and being aware of these will be useful for you as you face the challenges ahead. If you haven't already done so, a good first step is to identify where your weaker areas are (see Chapter 1). We all have weak areas – or areas in need of development, if you prefer – so working around these areas and, where possible, developing them will help you to become a strong and independent scholar in your field. Whilst the prospect of acquiring the skills that you need can appear daunting, with a little commitment and focus they will easily be within your grasp. What is required is realistic self-awareness, determination and self-control, and a clear plan. Of course, you will probably need guidance and support to help develop your study habits, but that does not mean that you have less control over your learning destiny. Being in control is about producing and executing a plan of action that will produce results. This is why you need to be aware of your existing strengths and limitations. Knowing where you are at present will enable you to identify where you want to be and how you will get there. This is your way of taking control and thus demonstrating your autonomy.

In higher education, autonomy is arguably a crucial component of success; indeed, it is often seen as one of the main goals of studying at this level (Fazey & Fazey, 2001). Autonomy in individuals can develop through independent experience and this is potentially a strength for many mature students, albeit they often do not perceive this to be the case (Henri et al., 2017). As an experienced individual, you may have many examples to draw on of situations in which you have used your initiative and have taken control and navigated through them. In this way, these experiences can be capitalised upon because you were acting autonomously. Of course, not all mature students can demonstrate amazing autonomy and independence, and even for those who do have more life experience than their peers, and thus a potential advantage, autonomy is usually a trait that is still being developed.

Whether you have an abundance of autonomy, then, or have yet to utilise its potential, you should think about the role you play in what you do. What aspects are you in charge of? Who do you rely on and what happens if they do not give you what you need? Most of us rely on other people or resources in our lives. Whether that is a loved one or a professional, or a particular service that we access, it is rare for someone to be totally self-sufficient and function individually. It is not unusual, then, to utilise your support mechanisms and still be considered to be autonomous. Being independent and in control does not mean being alone. It merely means that you can lead the way and can draw on the most appropriate support when needed.

Autonomy does not come easy for some people, and if you are one of those people you will have to be strategic in your approach. Firstly, you will need to be fully aware of the wider implications for your life and your studying. That is, what are you undertaking this degree for? What skills and knowledge do you need to succeed and what will you need to develop along the way? And what facilities do you have around you that can enable this process? As an autonomous individual, you will need to make decisions and carry them through, wherever possible. This requires planning and monitoring. Don't let someone do that for you, however, that is not autonomy. Of course, you can get help from other people, and as alluded to earlier, strong and independent people actually do this a lot. But they stay in overall control and guide those people into giving them what they want.

▶ TAKE CONTROL OF YOUR WORKLOAD

In Chapter 3 we discussed how you can manage your time and become self-organised and motivated. You should now use this experience to take full control of your learning journey. This is really useful for you as it gives you a clear sense of the direction of travel of your studies and means that you can identify key points along the way. Being in control means that you have an overview, as well, of all the factors involved. In this way, you can steer your workload in the direction that you want it to go in. Acting in this way may not come naturally to you, but you can work at it by establishing a range of strategies and ensuring that it is you who is making the key decisions. Whilst you do this, however, try to remain faithful to your own values and beliefs. If being in control makes you uncomfortable there are approaches you can take. One is that you can play a role – acting out that character who demands control of their learning – and distance your inner self from that role, thus executing a perhaps unfamiliar approach. As you become stronger in the role, however, you should find that your autonomy develops alongside. This can improve your chances of success. And more importantly, success will be measured by you and your standards, values, goals and so on. Playing a role is a useful way to transition into becoming autonomous, but at some point you should use it to develop personally as well, incorporating your newfound autonomy into who you are. This means that you should care more about yourself than anyone else does. It does not mean being selfish, of course; rather, it is about you taking control and thus having a hand in your own learning trajectory.

Autonomy for your assignments

As mentioned in earlier chapters, it is good practice when studying to say stay ahead of the game and thus start your work early. Having an early draft will allow you to get some feedback but it will also help you to reshape your writing and to rethink your argument (see also Chapters 8 and 10). You should ask yourself, is my draft strong enough? Have I been critical enough? Where can I improve? How does this reflect my objectives for this assignment? Having an early draft will ensure that you have time to address these questions effectively. The night before an assessment is due is arguably a poor time to be revising your paper, let alone to begin writing. If you are already feeling a little insecure as a mature learner, perhaps because it has been some time since you have studied, or because you are not fully confident in your ability yet, then this is even more reason to be strategic about your assignment. Tackle it early and prepare yourself to deal with any hurdles you may encounter along the way. In this way, you will be able to identify whether you are equipped to write your assignment yet or whether there is still a gap in your knowledge (more reading to do). You can't do this effectively the night before. As an autonomous individual you are in charge of the progress so it is up to you to work within a productive and plausible timescale.

▶ MOTIVATION

Some studies have shown that motivation can be a powerful contributor to success (e.g. Parker & Chusmir, 1991; Winter, 2010). Most of us know that if we are not motivated to do something it can be incredibly difficult, so it is perhaps easy to see that without motivation our goals are highly unlikely to come to fruition. This means that we are even less likely to take control of our actions if we have little commitment to them. We all need motivation. For instance, you may ask yourself what makes you get up in the morning. What is it that drives you from within and what are the external factors you covet? Why is going to university important for you and what do you hope to achieve? And importantly, why have you chosen to study your particular subject?

Motivation comes in all shapes and sizes, and whilst much of it is positive and beneficial, there are many occasions when the rationale for why and how we function is not fuelled by positive motivations. For example, supposing you had recently received a utility bill through your door, or you had a credit card statement that needed paying. It is likely that neither was not exciting for you but rather a mundane, if not somewhat irksome, task (nobody likes paying bills) that you were compelled to do. Whether you wanted to or not you knew it was the right course of action. You also decided to do it immediately to avoid forgetting, and justified that by stating, 'if it has to be paid then what is the point in waiting?' But what kind of motivation were you using to complete this task? It might have been neutral or negative but the reasons you held prompted you to act. In a similar manner, somebody completing an assignment that they are either not interested in or are almost out of time with might approach this with resentment. Aside from being poorly organised and unproductive, and generally functioning in a manner that can be detrimental to their health, these individuals are unlikely to be enjoying the experience. They are losing control and are seemingly motivated for the wrong reasons. A reactive response to a deadline can represent a negative rationale to be motivated, whereas a proactive response ensures that it is incorporated into a plan (see Chapter 3) and sustains autonomy. This need not (and arguably should not) be the case, however. If we spin this idea on its head, let's suppose that you are actually excited about your submission (bear with the idea). What would be the impact of this on your engagement with the assignment? As mentioned previously, there is no reason why you should not be excited about your studies. This is the subject that you chose and excitedly wanted to study, and it is the field in which you might demonstrate a level of expertise in the future.

However, it is understandable that this can be a difficult prospect to see. Let's rewind slightly, then, and try to pinpoint what is happening in relation to your motivation.

Motivation is often categorised as being either intrinsic or extrinsic (Deci & Ryan, 1985), albeit some theories suggest that it is multifaceted (Reiss, 2012) or that there is much overlap across the two, occurring on a continuum (Vallerand, 2000). For the purposes of clarity for this discussion, however, let's define the two terms distinctly. Intrinsically, you are driven by your inner desires. You love writing and perhaps want to be a prize-winning novelist so you enrol on a creative writing BA; you have a passion for acting so you are studying drama; you are fascinated by how societies function and want to understand them better so you read for a sociology degree. Or perhaps you were always good at maths and enjoyed learning how technology and the modern world works – hence, your pursuit of a *BSc in Engineering*. The common denominator across these examples is the subject interest or your individual passion. It aligns with your goals and reflects how you will fulfil your career aspirations. Intrinsically, then, you are incentivised by the potential to engage in what you like doing. Your extrinsic motivation for your study would relate to the external rewards that you hope you will achieve. For instance, it might lie in the necessity to have a degree in order for you to become an engineer or for you to study at a higher level to enter the job market at the point that suits you. Whilst both forms are not necessarily synergistic, and each drives you forward in its own specific way, they can be interrelated. Your intrinsic motivation can impact on your extrinsic motivation by identifying the need and relevance of a degree in relation to your end goal of working in that profession and thus engaging in what you love. On the other hand, your quest to acquire a respectable status within society might result in you pursuing a line of study that has been deemed necessary. For example, you want that high-paying job as a barrister and study law, even though it is not your first choice of subject. People often succumb to extrinsic motivation with career choices by ignoring something that could fulfil their dreams because the probability of succeeding in that field is low. This is a simplistic conception of these forms of motivation, of course, and as mentioned already they do interrelate. But it should be clear that motivation is impacting on us in different ways and for different reasons.

Sometimes our actions are fuelled by other negative motivations such as fear, and we might experience pain or loss if we do not act in a certain manner. For instance, you are forced to write a report over the weekend because you fear that not giving that report to your boss on Monday morning could jeopardise your position. The resultant action is the same but the reasons for doing so vary significantly. Where possible, of course, we would always benefit from being motivated in a positive way. Compare this experience with that of writing up a report for your boss that you are excited about and cannot wait for him/her to read it. To put this into a studying context, have a look at the example scenario below.

> Both Ranjid and Sarah have an assignment to write that is due for submission in one week. They have each done some preparation for this and both feel that they now just need to write up their notes into the template they have chosen. Sarah is negatively motivated, however, because she received a low grade for her previous work. She feels that she is struggling academically and that she will not be able to secure a good grade for this assignment, so she is not enjoying the experience. She merely wants to pass her degree so that she can get into paid employment. Ranjid, on the other hand, has a copious amount of notes from his reading and knows that his assignment can mostly be drafted from these. And feedback from Ranjid's previous assignment was overwhelmingly positive – the lecturer suggested that Ranjid 'should aim to publish some of his work as [he] writes really well and his works is mostly of a high standard.' Ranjid is now motivated extrinsically with the lure of seeing his name in print as well as with the possibility of securing a high grade. He is excited about this prospect and it also aligns with his intrinsic motivation to pursue an academic career like his parents. Unfortunately for Sarah, her lack of motivation is impacting on how much work she will put in. She becomes fixated with finishing her assignment merely to get it out of the

way so that she can do something more enjoyable. As a result, her assignment has become a chore, is seemingly much harder to write, and Sarah no longer cares what grade she will get.

At present, Sarah will not excel because there is too much distance between herself and her studies. She is not engaging with the subject and does not have a passion for it. Studying has also become a means to an end and Sarah is only motivated extrinsically, writing her assignment solely because she needs to pass it in order to obtain her degree. She could still be autonomous, of course, and that would be easier if her motivation was positively driven. However, it is driven by necessity rather than passion. Sarah is not intrinsically motivated so will probably complete the least amount of work that she feels she can get away with.

To resolve this, Sarah could inverse this thinking by engaging more with her reading and enjoying learning about her subject. She might even be lucky enough to have some choice in the assignment and thus write about a topic that she is particularly interested in. In this way, Sarah is identifying the positive factors as these can better motivate her (Deci & Ryan, 1985). She is also taking control of the assignment and reminding herself why she is doing her degree. As a result of these changes in her outlook, she may even become excited about writing her assignment. Effective autonomy requires commitment, and the more passionate and committed Sarah is, the more effective her autonomy will be. She will also have a greater oversight of her situation as her greater autonomy will cyclically lead to improved motivation. This is also reflected in Knowles's (1975, p. 14) claim that 'people who take the initiative in learning (proactive learners) learn more things and learn better than do people who sit at the feet of teachers, passively waiting to be taught (reactive learners).'

▶ LONG-TERM PLANNING

It is often difficult when you begin a university course to think about the long-term future. Your fixation for the present is likely to be on the degree, and that is highly understandable. Studying is perhaps a change of focus for you, a different career trajectory, a new life to get your head around. But long-term planning is very useful. After all, you probably have some long-term plans for what you want to do with your life which is why you have chosen to do a degree in the first place. The long-term plans are useful because they allow you to capture a fresh perspective of yourself. And you can use your specialist area of study to help you contemplate your future beyond your graduation. This is about taking control of your own destination and steering yourself towards that wherever possible. For some, doing a degree is merely the continuation of their schooling, and is something that they do because they like (or used to like) the subject. They have an interest in it but may not have thought about how this interest plays out into a career. As a mature student, however, you may be a step ahead in that you have actively chosen to move away from one particular route in life in order to pursue another. In this way, you have steered your life course onto another track and have thus already demonstrated some autonomy. It is not unusual, therefore, to think about the years ahead of you as both a student and then a professional with a clear career trajectory. To do this, let's look at some examples.

> Kelsey worked as a team leader in a large hotel that is part of a nationwide chain of hotels. She enjoyed her job for over three years but always dreamed of a change. Unsure of what to do she began to talk to some of her old friends from school. One was a police officer, one worked in accounting, and another was a primary school teacher. The teacher role appealed to Kelsey as she had always enjoyed working with children. Her keen interest in the development of her niece and nephew – alongside many weekends as a teenager minding them on numerous occasions – suggested to her that this might be an extremely rewarding profession. After chatting to her friend and gleaning as much information as she could, she enquired at her local primary school about the possibility of doing some voluntary support. This she did over a short period when on leave and she felt that in doing so she had found her passion. The sense of fulfilment she felt after each day left no room for uncertainty and from hereon Kelsey acquired as much knowledge as she could about

teaching. Just over a year later, and after being accepted onto a BA (Hons) course in her chosen university, Kelsey's wish was materialising as she about to embark on her initial teacher education pathway.

As a mature student, Kelsey had a clear career path in mind. She wanted to train as a primary school teacher and subsequently pursue opportunities for progression within this field. As a result of her team leading role in the hotel, Kelsey had experience in managing people and knew that this was an area of working that she was also keen to continue where possible. Thus, Kelsey had plans to move into senior leadership in later years. She believed that after her degree she would work as a teacher for several years and probably pursue an MA at some point, perhaps undertaking part-time study alongside her role. Kelsey felt that this would put her in good stead to look at management opportunities and, much later on, even leadership roles within the teaching profession. Her end goal was that of head teacher.

Kelsey was both insightful and ambitious when it came to knowing herself. She had reflected much on this during her time in her old job and even more so once she had identified her new career. Of course, not everybody can plan this far ahead, particularly when it requires moving into an unknown field. But doing so is both rewarding and productive and really hones your ability to demonstrate your autonomy. Having moved from a steady income to the investment of full-time study, Kelsey was keen to make the most of her time at university and to return to paid employment as soon as she could. Her previous employment experience meant that she already had an idea of what she wanted to do. Having also had several jobs before the hotel role, Kelsey was aware of many alternatives to her newfound profession and thus had the benefit of making an informed decision. Kelsey therefore capitalised on her mature student status, utilising her life experiences to maximise her potential. She was aware of her strengths as much as her weaknesses and strove hard to make them pay off. Kelsey came up against many life hurdles, of course, but throughout her journey she remained in control. Kelsey's motto was 'I have to take control because nobody will do it for me.' Next up we have George.

> George was also working full time but in a bank as a cashier. He had worked for the bank for five years and had undertaken numerous training courses in finance, fraud, and general banking procedures. However, George decided one day that the banking world was no longer for him. He wanted to return to full-time education, although he was unsure what he wanted to study. Having a strong interest in history, George looked into the possibility of doing a BA. Although he enjoyed learning about history, however, he had not yet contemplated where the degree could take him. Once he embarked on his studies, George realised that he had a lot of existing knowledge that he could draw on. His passion for the subject had led to much earlier reading and this was now standing him in good stead. As a mature student, George excelled in his studies, reading extensively and always submitting his work on time. Unfortunately for George, however, he left university with no clear direction. He had been confronted with several hurdles when seeking employment and had merely circumnavigated them using other people's advice. After returning to the bank for another two years and doing (almost) the same job that he had previously, George decided that he was not making the most of his degree by not working in his chosen field. He spoke to an adviser who helped him and George was steered towards some graduate schemes. After once again coming up against several hurdles, yet now being determined to overcome them, George put a lot more energy into finding the right job for himself. He became much more proactive in seeking vacancies and eventually this paid off as he secured a role as an archivist for a large organisation.

First, it must be said that George's lack of initial success does not reflect his chosen area of study. George could have saved himself a lot of time by planning for his future much earlier down the line. Whilst he benefited financially from his employment in the bank, it did set him back somewhat. The bank was not his first choice of career, yet he was hugely unfocused when he graduated and was thus swept along with the experience. George never regretted working in the bank, but he did wonder how his situation might have played out in a different way had he taken control of his learning trajectory whilst at university. Once he decided that he had had enough, George became much more focused and in control. His autonomy thus blossomed and today he is extremely happy in his archivist role and is thoroughly making the most of the link to his degree experience. George has even outlined some plans for how he can steer his career within the field of archivism over the next five years.

▶ BEING AN INDEPENDENT LEARNER

I shall finish this chapter with a brief discussion on independence in learning. This is an essential characteristic at postgraduate level but it is also one that you as a mature undergraduate should consider as you progress through your degree. In university you are given lots of opportunities to not only demonstrate your independent ability, but to actively use it to ensure success. This can be difficult as it is not always something that occurs in compulsory education. As a mature student of higher education, however, you may have a lot to bring to the table, much of which has previously been discussed. Your prior experience as an independent person, for instance, might mean that you have an advantage in becoming an independent learner. But being an independent learner requires much more than a mere proclivity to general independence. There will still be a lot of skills and knowledge you need to acquire in order to conduct your studies in an independent manner. As such, you should capitalise on your early university experiences and treat your autonomy and ability to be an independent learner as developing traits. For example, once you have completed your first assignment, you probably now have a template of sorts to drive your independent approach for the next one. You may also have experience now in areas such as searching for literature, collating and understanding that literature, synthesizing ideas, analysing data and presenting an interpretation of this analysis, working with others, structuring your assignment, writing academically, and defending your argument. This, and more, you can take to your next assignment as you develop an independent approach to studying. Take notes, therefore, and perhaps even keep a learning journal as this can be incredibly helpful for your thought processes and overall learning journey. Remember, you are not just learning more about your subject when you undertake a degree, you are moving into the world of academia and establishing a foundation as a professional in that area. As such, you should tailor your experience to facilitate your further development and keep control of your overall progress. In the next part we shall deal with some of the academic conventions that will be useful to you as an independent scholar, and we begin this in Chapter 5 with a discussion on the benefits and purpose of effective notetaking.

▶ REFERENCES

Deci, E. L., & Ryan, R. M. (1985). *Intrinsic motivation and self-determination in human behavior*. Plenum.

Fazey, D. M. A., & Fazey, J. A. (2001). The potential for autonomy in learning: Perceptions of competence, motivation and locus of control in first-year undergraduate students. *Studies in Higher Education*, 26(3), 345–361. https://doi.org/10.1080/03075070120076309

Henri, D. C., Morrell, L. J., & Scott, G. W. (2017). Student perceptions of their autonomy at University. *Higher Education*, 75(3), 507–516. https://doi.org/10.1007/s10734-017-0152-y

Knowles, M. S. (1975). *Self-directed learning: A guide for learners and teachers*. Association Press.

Parker, B., & Chusmir, L. H. (1991). Motivation needs and their relationship to life success. *Human Relations*, 44(12), 1301–1312. https://doi.org/10.1177/001872679104401204

Reiss, S. (2012). Intrinsic and extrinsic motivation. *Teaching of Psychology*, 39(2), 152–156. https://doi.org/10.1177/0098628312437704

Vallerand, R. J. (2000). Deci and Ryan's self-determination theory: A view from the hierarchical model of intrinsic and extrinsic motivation. *Psychological Inquiry*, 11(4), 312–318. https://www.jstor.org/stable/1449629

Winter, D. G. (2010). Why achievement motivation predicts success in business but failure in politics: The importance of personal control. *Journal of Personality*, 78(6), 1637–1668. https://doi.org/10.1111/j.1467-6494.2010.00665.x

5 The Art of Note-Taking

▶ INTRODUCTION

Students in higher education (HE) are often advised to take notes in class or in lectures, and there is an expectation – primarily because this is practice that continues from the traditional route to HE of studying A levels first – that you are not only aware of what this is, but that you will be proficient at it. But this is higher-level study and note-taking takes on a new significance. The requirement to be able to take notes can position some individuals, particularly those who have entered HE via one of the many different routes that are available, at a disadvantage. Whilst universities do offer support for study skills, what this looks like varies across institutions, with some experiencing high demand for it. This means that waiting lists for students can be several weeks, by which time you may have already missed the opportunity to utilise these skills in your lectures. Taking notes is an important skill and arguably an art form that represents the beginning of your academic engagement. This means that it goes beyond the mere recording of everything to identifying the salient points.

Taking notes is not merely an act of scrawling down comments on the décor of the room or the speaker's appearance, then, it is a process of engagement with the materials and of recording this in an accessible form for later use. Note-taking requires you to make connections between academic concepts, theoretical frameworks, innovative thinking, and your own understanding of the field. In many ways, note-taking represents the beginning of your own academic thought processes. To understand what this might look like in HE, let's begin with the traditional talk in the lecture hall, a practice that appears to date back to the Theatre of Dionysus in ancient Greece, around 500 BCE (Beichner, 2014).

▶ YOUR FIRST LECTURE

It is Monday morning and you have just arrived in the large lecture theatre. Your first experience of a lecture is about to get underway and you are a little nervous. You look around and everyone is chatting away and talking about the weekend. You have spoken to one or two people and hopefully you will be sitting next to someone you have already made contact with. If you are on your own, don't worry as you will need to concentrate on the lecture anyway. There are a mixture of people in the theatre. Some have notepads in front of them, others have laptops open and ready to go. They may all look prepared and you may even think that they are much further ahead than you but you should discard any such thoughts. Many will be excited yet apprehensive, and most will be unsure of how university life differs from studying at A-level. And as a mature student your transition to HE is likely to be similar for the majority of the students around you: starting a degree represents a new challenge in a new environment for everyone. However, as alluded to in previous chapters, many of your peers will not have your life experience as a mature student (even a small number of years can make a difference to how you see the world). And you should look upon this first lecture as a new chapter in your life story – the beginning of something great. After all, this is the subject you chose, the one that you are hopefully passionate about, and the study of which will hopefully result in the career of your choice. Take a few deep breaths, then, and turn that anxiety and nervousness into excitement. Now, let's get down to the mechanics of what you will do as you are sat enjoying the talk.

Note-taking is deemed to be critical for effective learning (Morehead et al., 2019) yet it can be a tricky business that you need to get right in order to maximise its benefits. Having a system of taking notes can not only save you time and help you to engage with the talk more profoundly, it can also enable you to return to these notes without seemingly reliving the whole lecture. But where do you start? Most novices will probably make the mistake of trying to note down everything that was said. And at this stage this is understandable as it is hard to say what will be important to you later on. You may not know what the module is about yet or where you will be steering your learning. However, you can still draw out some of the main messages of the talk and relate these to your existing knowledge of the subject. Rather than looking for direct relevance in the talk to an assignment, then, aim to engage with the areas in general to help you grow as a student of the field. For successful note-taking to occur, your aim for this talk is to glean an overall understanding of what is being argued – the gist, if you like – so that you are in a strong position to evaluate it and identify its relevance to you as a scholar.

▶ FOCUS ON THE GIST

Your first venture into note-taking might result in many scribblings that are potentially of little use if you are lacking a focus. This is why concentrating on the gist provides a foundation upon which you can later build complexity and add personal relevance. Some key questions to ask yourself are, 'what is the speaker telling us overall? What position are they taking? How does this build on what we know already?' Often, a speaker will express a point in many different ways or will reiterate the key messages several times. The speaker needs to get certain information across and this might be through repetition and paraphrasing, as well as presenting an argument or idea from different angles. What the speaker is doing here is encouraging you to think more deeply about the topic – what does it mean? What are the implications? How does the context contribute to the implications and the potential outcome of this idea? To give you an example of this, let's take a fairly simple concept of psychology: cognitive dissonance. Cognitive dissonance is a term to describe the process of holding contradictory thoughts or beliefs in your mind. For example, smokers may know that smoking is bad for them yet decide not to quit because they rationalize their behaviour in a way that identifies the supposed benefits of smoking. An example of attitudes to smoking can be seen in Box 5.1.

Box 5.1 Cognitive dissonance and smoking

In the UK, awareness of the damage of smoking is much clearer today for the wider society than it was before the smoking ban of 2007. And it is certainly much clearer than it was many decades ago when smoking was positively advertised and promoted and thus attractive for large swathes of the population. Indeed, you would be forgiven for thinking that nobody knew of the dangers of smoking before the 1940s – particularly as cigarettes were a favourite go-to-prop for many of the big screen legends such as Lauren Bacall, Humphrey Bogart, James Dean, and Rita Hayworth. But the dangers of smoking have actually been known for a very long time. In fact, a link between poor health and smoking was noted in a 1602 publication entitled *Work for Chimny-Sweepers or A Warning for Tabacconists* [sic] (Charlton, 2004). However, such dangers were largely ignored by the public or a justification was provided so that smokers could continue to engage in smoking in a guilt-free manner. But today most smokers know the dangers involved in what they do and, as such, have to wrestle with their cognitive dissonance.

Many modern-day health warnings have either prompted smokers to quit (Durkin et al., 2009; Lewis et al., 2015) or have acted as a deterrent for those considering whether to start smoking in the first place. Placing addictions aside for the present, however, those who choose to continue smoking may decide to generate a series of reasons for why they have chosen to do so (or why they are refusing to quit).

> Examples include, enjoying the moment, (ironically and erroneous) holding the belief that smoking is a mechanism for alleviating stress, and completely discarding the evidence for a 'let's just see what happens' approach to dealing with the risk. Smoking has also long been a social connector – witness those conversations that are sparked up (if you will pardon the pun) in the smoking shelter or just outside the building – and justifications are given in the form of mitigating the practice: 'I don't smoke often and I rarely go out socialising.' 'Cigarettes are my only vice.' These contradictory thoughts present dissonance for the individual and a choice has to be made in identifying which choice one will make.

In our psychology talk, then, let's imagine 'cognitive dissonance' was presented to the audience. The speaker provided examples and discussed the concept in much more detail, talking about the implications, the reasoning behind the creation of a rationale, the possible biochemical changes associated with smoking, and other contributions to the decision to smoke, such as addiction. The speaker also presented the nuances of some of the previous studies in this area. Your first attempt at taking notes, then, may look a little something like this:

> Psych. Cognitive dissonance. Holding two contradictory thoughts in our heads, such as justifying smoking despite understanding the consequences.
> *Example – I smoke but I don't drink [alcohol].* I don't take drugs and I eat healthily *(presumed balance).*
> Medical. Addictions and consequences. Rationale can grow, individual may smoke more and still justify it.
> Social. Links with motivation and impact on positive thinking. Impact on further morality/immorality.
> – Matthew Rabin paper of 1994

The notes here need to be meaningful, of course, and it might be that some points are not clear. This is worth considering carefully because when you return to these notes they need to make sense to you. For example, what is meant by 'rationale can grow'? You might know that this refers to the significance of the rationale but whether that would hold the same meaning in two months' time for you is another matter. You may decide to add a little sidenote on this, then, or revise it to 'rationale can become more complex as individual further justifies act.'

You may even choose to go beyond the discussion of the concept, perhaps identifying other examples that are meaningful to you, such as relating it back to your own learning journey and looking at justifications for any of your actions that have had adverse effects on it. You can subsequently reflect on these later and analyse them in order to better understand what is happening. The crucial aspect is to take notes that not only have meaning and relevance now but will also be useful to you when you return to them. And in doing so, you also need to ensure that they are concise enough for you to still be paying attention to what is being said – that is, don't spend all your time noting down one point only to miss several others in doing so. Had you recorded all or most of what the speaker said, it is likely that you will not have been able to process the concept in a meaningful way. This means that you are not really engaging in the lecture. This is the fine balance of note-taking, then, and you may find you need to practise it a few times before you perfect it.

Note-taking should enable you to glean important messages in a succinct manner, leaving you free to reflect on what is being discussed. This can be difficult to get right and some students may well leave the lecture theatre with pages and pages of writing yet have little to no knowledge of the ideas that were presented. Of course, if the notes are good they can revisit them and hopefully get to understand some of the complexity. But this is potentially not as effective because the 'thinking in the moment,' or what Schön (1991) calls reflection-in-action, opportunity has now gone. And the lecturer may not be available at this stage for you to ask questions. The balance, then, is to fully engage with the lecture yet to note down enough information for you to later return to, and understand, the arguments as effectively as you do now. And you can also follow up your notes with your reading.

Despite the necessity to record your engagement for posterity, however, you may find that some students have taken no notes at all, even if they engaged with the lecture throughout. Our memories are far from perfect – in fact they are highly flawed (see Shaw, 2017) – so it is likely that these students will forget much of this lecture over the coming weeks. Achieving the balance between engagement and recording, then, is important so let's move on to some other strategies for noting down your thoughts, particularly ones that will help you make sense of them at a later date.

▶ STRATEGIES

Headings help you to make sense of your notes and can be useful for showing coherence between points. You may even decide to draw a line to join some of the points where you see related areas, although it is helpful to briefly identify at the time what these connections are and mean. Headings enable you to categorise the information and thus add meaning to it. This is useful for drawing out themes in the talk. Why is the lecturer presenting this information? What is the relevance? How can I encapsulate the overall meaning? And perhaps, what is the connection between this and what I need to write about? You should be able to glean this information from the notes if you have used headings.

If these notes are contributing to the writing of an assignment, then later you may wish to use the sections to organise your draft so that it is sequenced appropriately. This helps you to design your structure and enables you to stay within your word count (See Chapter 10). What will the overall shape look like? Which sections need to be foregrounded – theoretical/conceptual frameworks, for instance? Which parts contribute to the discussion of your argument and thus will come later in the assignment? Which themes or sections of writing connect with others and why? In this way, you are shaping your thinking and this helps you to connect the lectures to the teaching sessions and to your independent study. In fact, you should actively look to make the connections between everything that you do in your studying (see Chapter 2).

It is important to make connections in your notes because concepts often do not function in a vacuum. They interrelate with other concepts and can vary in meaning, depending on the context. Making these connections helps to shape your thought processes. For example, using the earlier subject of psychology, you might be presented with research findings on motivation and decide that there is a connection here with cognitive dissonance. What motivates the person to give up smoking (or continue)? Is it intrinsic, extrinsic?

Underline key words or terms

Note where the information has come from – e.g. if your lecturer cites a particular study or the work of another academic you may wish to locate this later on. Is it based on fact? Was it merely their opinion or some anecdotal account from someone working in the field? This is important as you will need to validate the source and gauge its potential for making an academic contribution. At this point you may wish to use an asterisk to note an area to follow up. Key concepts can also be underlined as this helps them to stand out. In this way, you commit to using a layered approach to note-taking. That is, you can delve deeper into a concept – e.g. identify and analyse its component parts, draw links with other theorists' work, demonstrate relevance for other fields – and capture this as succinctly as possible. The example in Figure 5.1 illustrates how you might lay this out

When you return to your notes and you see that they sit under a heading, that some words or phrases are underlined, and that there are links to theorists and other fields, you should begin to recapture the nature of the lecture and thus get a picture of the key messages. As such, your notes should enable you to recreate the thought processes you had during the lecture and reconnect the links that you originally drew. Successful notes will also go

70 The Mature Student's Companion

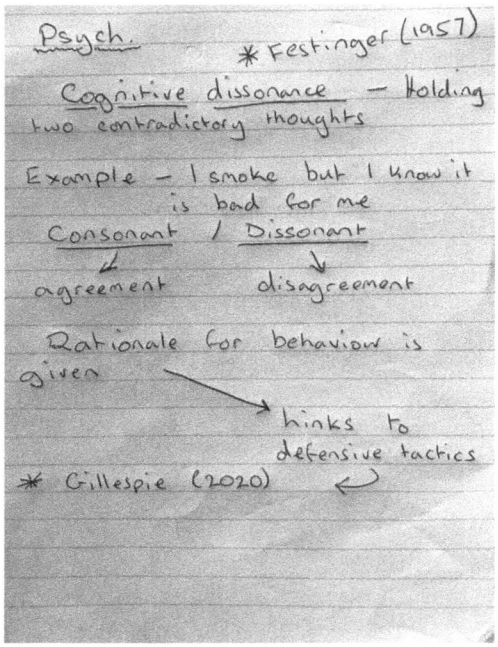

Figure 5.1 Recording your notes.

further than this, however, by generating opportunities to further explore the themes, so you should bear this in mind when listening. Ask yourself, where can I take this after the lecture? How do I follow it up? What evidence is available and where can I find it? This may be difficult at first but will develop with experience. As an example, your first action from the lecture might be to conduct a brief review of the literature in that area – i.e. find out what the research studies say about this topic. This is useful, regardless of what other actions you take as it gives you a fuller flavour of the topic. Also, use the key readings identified in the talk to steer you.

Discuss points with a friend where possible

Talking to a peer after a lecture is a useful way to improve your note-taking and to consolidate your knowledge, and it is a means for you to identify anything you may have missed. We all have our own interpretations of the world, so it is both useful and interesting to hear what another person made of the lecture. Their experiences will be different from yours so try to find out what resonated with them that may not have resonated with you. Why did they note something down as important when you have either glossed over it or missed it entirely? Of course, if you are working towards a particular assignment then note-taking in a lecture may look radically different from your peers, but where are the similarities? What can you learn from your fellow student's interpretation of the talk? Collaborating in this way can be both powerful and productive and will also help you in other areas of your studies, particularly where you need a confidence boost or reassurance.

Using a laptop versus note-taking by hand

Mueller & Oppenheimer (2014, p. 1166) found that 'participants using laptops were more inclined to take verbatim notes than participants who wrote longhand' which can impact on their potential to learn. However, they also reported that in one of their three studies 'longhand note takers outperformed laptop note takers on factual questions' and speculated that the reason for this 'may be that longhand note takers engage in more processing than laptop note takers' (Mueller & Oppenheimer, 2014, p. 1166). Indeed, findings from Askvik et al. (2020) support this, suggesting that handwriting can engender more effective learning through its impact on neurological processing. It would seem that handwriting has the edge, but it is perhaps more accurate to say that the jury is still out there and that much more research is needed in order to identify the most effective method (Cojean & Grand, 2024). There are clear pros and cons to using a laptop to take notes, and in-class use adds a different dynamic to note-taking in a lecture due to the necessity to contribute to the learning, so it is probably fair to say that choice is merely a matter of taste. Whilst using a laptop will work for many, for others it will be quite restricting and/or distracting (Kraushaar & Novak, 2010).

This is a personal choice, then, and as a stimulus to get you thinking about it and possibly help you to decide, Table 5.1 contains six

TABLE 5.1 Notetaking methods

Using a laptop

Strengths	Weaknesses
Notes can be edited – deleted, changed etc.	Requires minimum typing ability for speed
Notes can be reorganised	Pop-ups (e.g. adverts, notifications) can be distracting
Different colour fonts can make text stand out	May need a power source (i.e. battery is low)
Notes can be shared (emailed back to yourself)	Temptation to transcribe the lecture, i.e. to type the spoken word of the lecture in verbatim
Notes can be stored on a cloud/hard drive (easily accessible)	Electronic devices can fail
MS Word options (e.g. cut and paste) help to avoid duplication in writing and are less time consuming	Cost (initial outlay).

By hand

Strengths	Weaknesses
Instant hard copy of the notes	Notes cannot be shared (although they could be photocopied, depending on clarity of handwriting)
No reliance on technology	Duplication cannot be avoided (e.g. repeatedly writing down a term or phrase)
Can draw quickly, e.g. arrows across the page to connect themes	No immediate storage of the document
Does not depend on typing ability	Exhaustion – hand may tire (also, make sure you also have a spare pen)
No distractions	Notes are taken separately and thus connections have to made later through comparisons of each set of notes
Longhand notes may generate more elaborate 'brain connectivity patterns' (Van der Weel & Van der Meer, 2024)	Quotes or interesting pieces of information that may be needed for an assignment will probably need to be typed out later on

generic pros and cons for each approach (there are, of course, many others). Once you have decided on your preferred method of note-taking, you should consider the following questions carefully: What am I going to do with these notes? Will they be used for writing later on (e.g. an assignment)? Are they an aide memoire for me to return to when revising for an exam? Or do they represent the start of a deep exploration in that area? This final question might relate to an area that you are interested in and wish to consider taking forward for a project or assignment focus, should such choice be available.

▶ NOTE-TAKING HELPS YOU TO REMEMBER

Whilst you are taking notes, you are going over the ideas in your head and finding a way to record these in a succinct manner. This means that there is much thinking involved and thinking is essential in academia. This is also why it is not good practice to try to take down everything that was said as that would overload your cognitive capacity to process the event in any meaningful way. Taking notes in such a robotic form, which actually isn't note-taking but more of an attempt at transcribing the whole lecture, is of little use (Mueller & Oppenheimer, 2014). It prevents or limits you from reflecting on the ideas that are presented to you. Noting down your thoughts and key points that have arisen, perhaps also with some relevant themes, is the beginning of your cognitive engagement with your subject, and this should have multiple culmination points (usually in the form of assignments). These are known as summative assessments and are used by your tutors to apply a measurement to your knowledge of a particular area. Note-taking is part of this process because you are already grappling with ideas and making sense of the input by reformatting it – i.e. writing down the crux of what was said and noting any implications. If something has prompted you to think, even without referring to your notes you might recall where that information first came to you because the experience was meaningful –you were engaged with the ideas at the time and your notes indirectly influenced your thinking. Your notes then bolster this thinking by providing a foundation for you to return to, such as when revising for an exam.

Our memories thrive on key events and repetition is a way of telling our brains that certain information is important. Listening to the lecture, reflecting on the potential meaning for our personal goals and then writing down what was said and why it is important, provides our brains with multiple stimuli in relation to the same information. In this way, we reaffirm what we are told. We collate the information and make individually meaningful sense from it. This is one of the reasons why assessments are used. Not only do they form a crucial mechanism for tutors to record your progress and measure this against the performance indicators, an assessment requires you to read, think, and write about an area, thus causing your brain to engage with an issue in several different ways. Working towards an assignment mimics an in-depth exploration of a particular issue and thus encourages you to consolidate your knowledge. If done well, assignments enable you to progress with your knowledge of the subject and hopefully take a personal interest in wanting to find out more. Thus, assignments should make you hungry for learning and you should feel proud when you are writing up an assignment that demonstrates your knowledge. To do this well, you need to get into a positive and productive habit of note-taking. And the process is cyclical as preparing for an assignment also helps you to sharpen your note-taking (remember the key message that everything is connected?). This means that your overall progress should improve as you progress through the academic year.

Don't skip lectures and take your own notes

It may be tempting (but we would be naïve to think that it had never happened) to ask a friend to take notes for you. Perhaps you cannot attend the lecture due to an illness. This is unavoidable and in this instance is the next best thing. However, missing a lecture merely because your friend will take notes or not taking any at all because you will merely look at what the person next to you wrote down is a sure way of missing a trick in your learning.

As already argued, note-taking contributes to your thinking processes, and as you have missed this your friend's notes will then need to be interpreted. Apart from the distinct lack of impact on you personally (you were not there to understand the talk and put the notes into your own words), these notes will likely have only focused on what your friend was interested in. Where possible, then, ensure that you attend and engage in your lectures as they equate to much more than just a series of notes.

▶ ESTABLISH GOOD PRACTICE FOR PREPARING FOR YOUR EXAMS

Taking notes is not only a skill in identifying and recording the crucial information in a lecture, it is also about deciding what is, and will be, important for you moving forward for other assessments, such as an exam. In preparing for exams, you will be expected to draw up a set of notes that you can rely on as a study aid. In a way, this is a condensed form of information that is much more accessible than reading through journal articles and books and watching lectures over and over again. Your notes are thus a precis, a summary of the corpus of information, consisting of the key points you will need to regurgitate in your exam, and your notes can also be a useful way of avoiding plagiarism. For instance, you may have read of a great idea but have forgotten where that idea came from. It would be easy in this situation to accidentally pass off this information as your own if you have no traceable record. And even if this is unintentional, you have still plagiarised. At best it is careless and demonstrates that you are not as familiar with your subject as you should be.

Plagiarism carries heavy penalties of academic misconduct and each university has its individual take on how to deal with this. It is a serious offence and can lead to your compulsory withdrawal from a programme. Taking notes with a record of the full citation helps you to avoid this. And even if you do recall that you read about this idea and intend to cite it, it may be extremely difficult to track down the source some weeks, and even months, later.

Why spend hours scouring the internet for a citation when you could be doing something much more productive with your time? The old adage of 'fail to prepare, prepare to fail' is relevant here, and if your notes are detailed enough they will enable you to use them to make the most of your learning.

Learn to be critical

The above principles also apply to note-taking when reading, of course, and the interaction with the text is similar because what you are reading is the equivalent of the author speaking. Note-taking helps you to focus on what is important in your reading and thus develops your criticality. Don't be afraid to challenge things when you hear or read them. Your notes will record your journey of engagement and will support you as you develop your thinking. And as you read more widely, you will slowly learn the art of criticality (see Chapter 8). It is about wanting to know more and not accepting everything that you hear or read, even if it comes from a printed source or an expert in the field. You can challenge anything as long as you have evidence. Where you do not have evidence – but mere gut instinct – you should tread wisely. Being tentative is a good approach, even with evidence, as it shows you are open-minded. Strong arguments invariably have counter arguments, some stronger than others. Nevertheless, there is usually something to make you think differently. You should engage with these in order to broaden your horizons and thus to understand a position more strongly. And this journey often begins with your note-taking – recording interesting points, useful quotes, challenging ideas, innovative strategies and so on. Your notes should thus become much more extensive as you progress because you should keep adding to them. In this way, you develop a critical eye and use your notes to record your progress.

Note-taking on a piece of text

When note-taking on an academic source, the principle described above is very similar. However, there is a minor difference in that you are not recording what was said, but merely commenting on it. The following extract is from Paulo Freire's (Freire, 1970) seminal text in the field of education, *Pedagogy of the Oppressed* and it contains notes representing an interpretation of the narrative. There are seven comments on this extract alone, each relating to an area that is underlined. Whilst this may appear to be a lot of comments for such a small extract, it is merely to exemplify the sorts of points you might wish to make. The notes may represent themes that could be explored, ideas that should be developed, or questions that need to be addressed. Each note should provide a stimulus for further thinking.

> The oppressed suffer from the duality which has established itself in their innermost being. They discover that without freedom they cannot exist authentically.[1] Yet, although they desire authentic existence, they fear it.[2] They are at one and the same time themselves and the oppressor whose consciousness they have internalized.[3] The conflict lies in the choice between being wholly themselves or being divided; between ejecting the oppressor within or not ejecting them; between human solidarity or alienation; between following prescriptions or having choices;[4] between being spectators or actors;[5] between acting or having the illusion of acting through the action of the oppressors; between speaking out or being silent, castrated in their power to create and re-create, in their power to transform the world.[6] This is the tragic dilemma of the oppressed which their education must take into account.[7]

1. Inner turmoil
2. The role of fear in education?
3. Self-perpetuating trauma
4. Autonomy
5. Activism or complicity?
6. Wider societal impact
7. Is education political?

Notes such as these can be made in a variety of ways and if you are taking notes on the PDF of a journal article there are tools within the PDF reader (e.g. Adobe) that can assist you, including opportunities to highlight key words and sentences or to type in a comment on the text itself.

▶ REFLECT ON YOUR PROGRESS

Reflection is a powerful tool and it is one that you already have within your arsenal. You should start this process after the first set of notes you have taken. Wait for some time so that the notes are not as fresh in your mind – perhaps a few days – and then come back to them to see how effective they really are. Can you recapture the flavour of the lecture or article you read? Are they meaningful and useful for you to reflect on? What is missing? Perhaps you noted a term but did not include the context. Or maybe one of your sentences does not make sense and you have forgotten why you wrote it. This happens from time to time but can hopefully be avoided by following the advice in this chapter. Reflection helps you to see that note-taking is not really something that starts at the door of the lecture hall, or when you open that text book, and finishes when the lecture is over or the book has been closed. You should have a written record of your thoughts, your ongoing conversation with yourself, and ideas you have as you progress.

We all reflect at different times in our lives, some more deeply than others, and many of us have to think through some extremely difficult and complex situations. If you are really conscientious, you may wish to keep a diary of your progress. This is a great way to monitor your development and when you are feeling as if you are not getting anywhere you can look back on how far you have come and how much you have achieved. Many of us like to situate ourselves within the competitive field and understand where we are in relation to others. Am I behind? Am I ahead of the game? What do I need to catch up on? Which areas am I actually leading on and how could these form themselves into future strengths – i.e. what do I want to be known for? A diary of your progress tracks your educational journey and can help you to identify the areas you need to work on. In this way, the progress you have made through your studies is available for you to revisit and you can use this to help you develop further. For example, suppose you have been reading for an assignment and taking notes. Your reflective diary will enable you to track the sources (papers and books) you have read and to collate the notes you have made. It records your thinking process and enables you to see how that develops over time. What questions did you ask and why? What did you note as important and why? If done well, it is likely you will look back on this diary in a year or two and see how you have grown.

Although seemingly time consuming, a reflective diary is arguably a wise investment of your efforts and could actually save you a lot of time in the future. Supposing your next assignment builds on previous study. Your notes and reflective diary will provide a foundation for you to draw on, thereby cutting down some of the preparation time. This is thinking like a true scholar. It is paving the future in a way that establishes you as a specialist in your field. After all, a degree is not merely a tick-box exercise that some may see it as. It is the establishment of a foundation of knowledge within a body of information, a foundation upon which you will continue to develop and grow as you progress in your career. Note-taking, therefore, is not merely something that gets you through an assignment or an exam. It is the key to establishing a knowledge base and thus the building blocks of successful study.

▶ CONCLUSION

There are many difficulties when taking notes but some of the common ones include recording information that is irrelevant, taking extensive notes that prevent you from engaging in the lecture, missing key points (perhaps you are not sure what is useful and what is not), and making illegible scrawls on the page that seemingly make sense when you record them but will be of no use later on. Moreover, many students never return to their notes, but this is clearly a weakness in their approach to learning. They either miss out on much information or they have to capture it again somewhere else.

It is also easy to miss important information if you are trying to write down everything so focus on only capturing the salient points. This means you have to make a decision on what is potentially important and what you can afford to perhaps forget. This will develop with practice and will become easier as you get to know your course. Once you have completed your first assignment, for instance, you will have a greater understanding of the topics of study and the expectations of your academic writing. However, if you are really new to note-taking it might even be useful for you to seek training in a specialist system, such as shorthand. This enables you to capture the key points of a lecture but still engage with the content. For reading, of course, you have the advantage in that the text can be re-read several times. Working at your own pace is thus crucial and even just beginning with basic bullet points (avoiding full sentences) is a useful strategy to adopt. And from there you can develop the complexity of your notes. Whether you are an experienced note-taker, then, or a novice, utilising the principles discussed above should facilitate a smooth and effective route to successful note-taking. In the next chapter we will build on this discussion by examining what it means to engage in critical reading.

▶ REFERENCES

Askvik, E. O., van der Weel, F. R. (Ruud), & van der Meer, A. L. H. (2020). The importance of cursive handwriting over typewriting for learning in the classroom: A high-density EEG study of 12-year-old children and young adults. *Frontiers in Psychology, 11*. https://doi.org/10.3389/fpsyg.2020.01810

Beichner, R. J. (2014). History and evolution of active learning spaces. *New Directions for Teaching and Learning, 2014*(137), 9–16. https://doi.org/10.1002/tl.20081

Charlton, A. (2004). Tobacco or health 1602: An Elizabethan doctor speaks. *Health Education Research, 20*(1), 101–111. https://doi.org/10.1093/her/cyg097

Cojean, S., & Grand, M. (2024). Note-taking by university students on paper or a computer: Strategies during initial note-taking and revision. *British Journal of Educational Psychology*. https://doi.org/10.1111/bjep.12663

Durkin, S. J., Biener, L., & Wakefield, M. A. (2009). Effects of different types of antismoking ads on reducing disparities in smoking cessation among socioeconomic subgroups. *American Journal of Public Health*, 99(12), 2217–2223. https://doi.org/10.2105/ajph.2009.161638

Freire, P. (1970). *Pedagogy of the oppressed*. Bloomsbury Academic.

Kraushaar, J., & Novak, D. (2010). Examining the effects of student multitasking with laptops during the lecture. *Journal of Information Systems Education*, 21(2), 241–252.

Lewis, S., Sims, M., Richardson, S., Langley, T., Szatkowski, L., McNeill, A., & Gilmore, A. B. (2015). The effectiveness of tobacco control television advertisements in increasing the prevalence of smoke-free homes. *BMC Public Health*, 15(1). https://doi.org/10.1186/s12889-015-2207-2

Morehead, K., Dunlosky, J., Rawson, K. A., Blasiman, R., & Hollis, R. B. (2019). Note-taking habits of 21st century college students: Implications for student learning, memory, and achievement. *Memory (Hove, England)*, 27(6), 807–819. https://doi.org/10.1080/09658211.2019.1569694

Mueller, P. A., & Oppenheimer, D. M. (2014). The pen is mightier than the keyboard: Advantages of longhand over laptop note taking. *Psychological Science*, 25(6), 1159–1168. https://doi.org/10.1177/0956797614524581

Rabin, M. (1994). Cognitive dissonance and social change. *Journal of Economic Behavior & Organization*, 23(2), pp.177–194. https://doi.org/10.1016/0167-2681(94)90066-3

Schön, D. A. (1991). *The reflective practitioner: How professionals think in action*. Routledge.

Shaw, J. (2017). *The memory illusion: Why you might not be who you think you are*. Anchor Canada.

Van der Weel, F. R., & Van der Meer, A. L. H. (2024). Handwriting but not typewriting leads to widespread brain connectivity: A high-density EEG study with implications for the classroom. *Frontiers in Psychology*, 14. https://doi.org/10.3389/fpsyg.2023.1219945

6
How to Engage in Critical Reading

▶ THE LITERATURE

You may hear mention of 'the literature' a lot in higher education (HE) so it is good to know exactly what is meant by this. Some use it to refer specifically to classic texts: for example, the works of Austen, Steinbeck or Wilde. This is evidenced through degree programmes that offer bespoke areas, such as 'English literature,' 'American literature' or 'Irish writing.' Some use the term to refer to informative guides, such as an information leaflet in a medical centre. Others see everything that has been written as literature. They are all right in their own way as literature can be all of these things. And this means that a typical tabloid is as much to be considered as a piece of literature as the works of Tolstoy or an article in the British Medical Journal. Intellectually, however, we hold that these sources vary significantly in quality and have different purposes.

From an academic perspective, the term literature represents the findings of research that have been written up for publication. So, if you are studying biology, it would refer to the published scientific articles and reference texts that are available in that particular field. And within this, you might also allude to the literature on 'the eye' or 'the ear' as separate bodies of evidence. The reference texts we draw on – journal articles, textbooks, organisational magazines and so on – are the academic go-to sources. And in academia these are also ranked hierarchically. International, peer-reviewed journal articles in a reputable journal tend to be ranked highest. These are not flawless by any means, and there is a whole host of writings on the elitism of this and the challenges it brings, along with the subsequent marginalisation effect on other writings. For now, however, these are the best that we have and to understand why this is considered so, we should briefly explore the publishing process.

The public domain

Research that has been conducted robustly and under ethical clearance from a reputable institution needs to be disseminated, and this is typically done through publication in a journal. This is viewed as the 'gold standard' of publications, providing it has been peer reviewed. That is, the submitted manuscript is scrutinised and reviewed by reputable researchers in the field. These reviewers (usually academics with a PhD or equivalent) hold knowledge of the field. That is, they are aware of the current understanding of the field and what direction it is heading in. They are familiar with the key studies and they know the subject well as a whole. Their knowledge is current as they are reading and researching in this area themselves. These people, then, are seen to be best positioned in which to judge the academic rigour and intellectual contribution of research studies.

Only once the gatekeepers (reviewers and editors) agree is a paper placed in the public domain as a journal article. The process runs a little like this: The editor of the journal first screens the paper – is it suitable for the readership of the journal? Does it look well written and present a robust argument? Is it a well-executed study that has key messages that move the field on? If the answer to these is yes, it is sent out to two or three reviewers. The reviewers then make a recommendation – reject it, accept it, or ask the authors to revise it and then resubmit it. This process of review can go through several iterations – e.g. the authors amend it, the reviewers suggest it is not finished, the authors revise it again etc. – although an editor will likely end the process if the authors are not seen to be cooperating fully or a paper is just not developing. This is usually done in the best interests of the journal and the whole process itself is conducted with criticality.

Once the paper is accepted, it goes to production – copyediting, typesetting and so on – and will eventually be published online and (if available) in a print copy. The article will also have global appeal and hence will speak to an international audience. In this way, it is accessible to, and cognisant of, the wider body of knowledge. So that is how the 'gold standard' article comes to be available to scholars and students. But what does it all mean?

The articles referred to above are the literature and are the product of large academic debates. At least, that is a simplistic but useful way to conceptualise them. Each discussion/debate is our current knowledge of the field – what we already know and thus do not have to resort to finding out for ourselves. When anything is challenged or added to that body of knowledge, it is done so through the form of another paper. For many years, the academic debate was exactly that – a toing and froing between academics, with the occasional outsider contributing but the general public never really being privy to the debate. Findings would eventually filter through to the public, via journalism or academic presentations, but some were misrepresentations that the public was not able to verify. This was because articles were behind paywalls and only available to institutions (usually HEIs) that subscribed to them. This is still the situation for the most part, although the landscape is changing with a variety of open access options, the use of Creative Commons licences, and alternative means of dissemination in the modern world, such as accessible media outlets. Other forms of literature include books, magazines and blogs, as well as numerous outputs on websites, the quality of which will vary. What you are doing, then, when you look for the literature is searching for some evidence-based information. For instance, what do we currently know about this topic? To answer this, we find and read the literature.

Sourcing your literature

For many of your assignments, you will need to draw on the literature and at some point you might be required to write a literature review, either as a stand-alone piece of work or as a section within your assignment. This involves getting together a collection of sources and reviewing them – i.e. reading them, pulling out the key points, and synthesizing your findings. In other words, what do the studies tells us? How do they perceive or approach the problem differently? What conflict or agreement can we identify between the studies? What do we make of them as a whole? This is your literature review. A useful and easy place to start your search is your essential reading list for the module. This will signpost you to the types of literature that you are expected to be reading, and it is a good start because someone has already collated relevant sources for you. But this is not an exhaustive list, and for your assignment you will need to read more widely. A recommended reading list might also be available to guide you, but these are usually noted as 'indicative.' As you are encouraged to become an independent scholar, then, this means that you should seek other sources as well.

To identify the appropriate sources, your university will have some form of search engine within its library that you can access online. Google Scholar is also useful these days. And you have a range of databases that you may wish to access. There is no point listing them all here as it will depend on your field, but examples include databases such as *Psychinfo* (behavioural and social sciences) and *PubMed* for biomedical sources. Once you have all your sources, your next job is reading. If they are journal articles – and most should be so that you can get a reliable and current grasp of the field – you will have an abstract for each. The title of your article may indicate what the content is likely to focus on – i.e. if it is useful for you – but many of these are incredibly unreliable. The abstract is a precis of the study and should tell you a little more. Some are written to illustrate the findings whilst others have more of a cloak-and-dagger approach, almost like a murder mystery where the author is afraid of giving away the ending. Regardless of the format, the abstract should tell you whether the whole article is worth reading. As with the title, you will need to make a judgement call. But it is usually an indicator of the potential content.

Snowballing

One method of finding more sources is to snowball. This involves looking at the reference list of an article that you have used and seeing who the authors have cited. If we see the literature as one big academic conversation, then it makes sense to ask yourself who the contributors are. You can do this many times, even with the extra articles you find, but it is important to remember that you are currently going backwards in time (i.e. your sources are getting older each time). This is great for an historical overview of how the arguments originated and have evolved, but at some point you will need to project forward to ascertain more current knowledge. Fields change, some quicker than others, so it is important to keep your knowledge up to date and to ensure that what you are writing about represents the most recent understanding of this area. As such, it is a good rule of thumb for the majority of your sources to emanate from the last five years (albeit this really depends on the nature of your search). And you may also need to include seminal texts – sources that have had a profound effect on the field.

You can find newer sources by snowballing forward. To do this, put the details of the article (a DOI is good) into Google Scholar. This will generate a number of hits and you will see that each entry has clickable links underneath it: e.g. 'save', 'cite', and so on. Locate your article on the page and click on the 'cited by' option. This will open up all the sources that have cited that article and is an indication of where the conversation has moved to. And you can repeat the process with your newer sources. In fact, the whole process is cyclical so you can keep going backwards or forwards with your sources until you have the all articles you require. There are limitations to this, however, in that you are only locating articles that have been cited, so you should use this approach in conjunction with your earlier searches (Box 6.1).

Box 6.1   FAQs

How many sources do I need?

Apart from saying 1,000 is too many and 1 is too few, this is a very difficult question to answer. You are not expected to review every text that has been produced for that topic, particularly if it is just a section in your paper or assignment. Your review of the literature should take into account some of the key texts (use the system described in the main text to identify and locate these) and the central arguments that have been posed. It is not an exhaustive record of the field. Even a systematic literature review or a meta-analysis will have limits and will use a rationale for why the authors have not included certain articles. This may seem like cherry picking, and to an extent it is, but you must try to distance yourself as much as possible and take an objective look at the literature. Too many sources mean that you need to narrow the parameters of your search or your hits. As a ballpark figure (and this is nothing other than this and, in many ways, meaningless) you might have around 20–30 sources in a 5,000-word article. It all depends on how you engage with them, however. And if you find yourself merely dropping one or two in for the sake of it, consider their impact and what the assignment would say if they were removed. Would it alter the central argument? What do they bring to the table? It is better to engage more with your sources than to include lots of sources that are empty and meaningless.

> ### What if I have a really old source? Should I discard it?
>
> Not necessarily. Is it a seminal text (see main narrative)? Does it make a key contribution and is it necessary to cite that author – e.g. they are the founder of a particular theory? Do consider what has been written since then, however. You might be training to be a teacher and include a source on brain gym, for instance, or learning styles, only to find out later that these areas have been heavily critiqued and debunked.
>
> ### Do policies count?
>
> Yes, albeit these are often what we term as grey literature. The policy stance is important for context but do bear in mind that some will make bold statements that you would need to verify with the literature of the field.

▶ CRITICALITY

When we look at something at face value, we do so simplistically. For criticality, however, we need to examine its complexity, embrace its breadth and depth, and explore its multi-faceted nature. You may have heard of the term criticality or some of its related forms applied to an activity – e.g. critical writing, critical reading. These are different instances of engaging in criticality. But what does it mean to be critical? Most of us will have an idea of this term when we use it; for instance, we are critical of a friend's dress sense or the way they behave, meaning that we disapprove of these things. In academia, however, the term is a little more than that. Yes, we might be looking for a criticism in the sense of disagreement, but we are also evaluating that item – identifying its strengths and weaknesses. We are thus scrutinising it to see how it measures up. Let's go back to our dress sense example, then, to see how this works. Your friend Brian is wearing his favourite shoes that you believe do not align with his choice of jeans. You can critique his dress sense by suggesting that those shoes just do not go with those jeans. But let's look a little deeper than that. Why is there a clash? What is wrong with the shoes/jeans? Are they both wrong? Should one pair go whilst the other one stays? Let's suppose that Brian is not blissfully unaware of his apparent faux pas but is actually comfortable in, and confident with, his choice of attire. Brian rejects societal impositions of 'fashion' and somebody else's decision that one item of clothing cannot be matched with another. Your friend is not wrong, merely of a different opinion to an influential majority and thus employing a critical approach. Brian may also present a rationale to suggest that his outfit is practical for his chosen activity for today, or that his alternative footwear would have actually caused problems for him.

We are now beginning to see the bigger picture and that the situation is not clearly one-sided. Let's go further and imagine that Brian has administered a poll to two hundred random men regarding a choice of footwear and found that the majority matched up the same shoes and jeans in the way that Brian did. Brian now has statistical evidence to support his argument, but that still doesn't mean that you were initially wrong in your opinion or that Brian is now correct. Whilst he has applied a critical approach, we too need to be critical of this by examining his methods and his evidence. A survey is a valid method of gathering data, but suppose his survey was administered to a particular demographic; for instance – all men of a certain age. Does this add another dimension to the evidence? The scenario demonstrates that there are many factors to consider in matching items of clothing, and what Brian has in his favour is evidence to argue that his fashion choice is not out of the ordinary as it resonates with the tastes of others. But this might not be proof and it may still leave him open for us to argue that the two clothing items conflict.

Of course, criticality in academia is much more than arguing over the most suitable shoes to wear. But in a similar way it does require alternative perspectives and theories to be discussed, and evidence to be evaluated. When we are critical, we don't accept things on face value. We want evidence, opinions, robust rationales and so on. We also want to hear the contrary argument, without which you could claim we can't really state that we have such a strong argument in the first place as we don't know the alternatives. The contrary argument also highlights to us the assumptions that were made when the initial argument was constructed, i.e. certain shoe styles and colour need to align with certain types of denim trousers. So, our first assumption that Brian is 'wrong' and that fashion is 'right' is more complex. Let's look at some academic examples and the use of theory.

Using theory

Sometimes you don't need to 'reinvent the wheel' as there are lots of theories in existence that we can utilise. Each tells us that many people before us have investigated this particular phenomenon and have drawn on evidence to explain how we could understand it in a particular way. To engage in criticality, then, we may wish to align ourselves with a theory and explore how this theory can provide explanations. For example, William Shakespeare is regarded as a true literary genius whose works have surpassed many others in depth, creativity and aestheticism. He is often quoted as the greatest literary figure who ever lived, and over the centuries we have seen various schools of thinking applied to his works. Critical theories have explored his characters through a range of frameworks; for example, using psychological concepts such as self-determinism, motivation, and resilience to provide a rationale for behaviour. Or, through sociological perspectives – applying a Marxist reading to the role of mercenary and avaricious merchants within society (Shylock). Or even through a philosophical lens, such as the debate on why Hamlet deliberates for so long on what to do about avenging his father's death yet impulsively and irrationally stabs at a moving arras (curtain) and inadvertently kills Polonius.

In this way, there are a wide range of perspectives available and multiple lenses that can be used for analysis. And as societies and cultures progress, attitudes change and understandings develop and transmogrify. Indeed, Shakespeare's Shylock, from the *Merchant of Venice*, was once perceived to be a 'victim-hero' before subsequent scholars dismissed this and deemed him a villain (Cooper, 1970). Changes are not always linear and progressive, of course, and scholars argue that many areas have actually regressed. However, the main point is that change occurs and with it brings new perspectives, many of which we may need to get our heads around. And utilising criticality in this example does not necessarily mean that you have to accept the profundity of Shakespeare's works. You may dismiss his writings altogether, perhaps argue for more contemporary literature to take the forum, or even problematise the whole concept of hierarchical forms of literature. This is criticality – it knows no bounds and pushes thinking wherever possible. And this is what is required from university study. And as a mature student you may have some experience of people applying different perspectives and even perhaps how knowledge is constructed. How do people claim to know things, for instance, and what constitutes their evidence?

Proposing and utilising theories is a way of unpicking the complexity of a phenomenon as a theory establishes a framework for understanding. But where this presents conflicting understandings (as is often the case), there is a necessity to adopt a critical stance and identify the limitations. Theories do not have to clash and multiple perspectives can work where there is congruence. However, such resolution might involve a reframing of the theory to fit the current understanding. This is how theories themselves can develop and change. Conflict typically results from a 'who is right and who is wrong?' approach. But criticality demonstrates complexity, and complexity is not an easy construct to frame. Often, each side has both elements of accuracy and inaccuracy and might represent different ways of experiencing the same phenomenon. Your job, then, as a student with a critical approach to reading, is to examine the arguments, synthesize the evidence, and produce a fully substantiated interpretation that you are confident can be robustly defended. And in the next chapter, we will move on from this to explore how you can rigorously construct an argument.

▶ REFERENCE

Cooper, J. R. (1970). Shylock's humanity. *Shakespeare Quarterly*, *21*(2), 117–124.

7 Constructing an Argument

▶ WHAT MAKES A GOOD ARGUMENT?

According to the online version of Merriam-Webster (2024), an argument is 'a reason for or against something.' That is, it is a position that someone proposes and defends. Building on this, Epstein (2018, p. 5) defines an argument as 'an inference that is intended by the person who sets it out to convince someone…that the conclusion is true'. In this way, an argument is presented as valid and the listener is urged to accept it. For some, presenting a convincing argument requires confidence and conviction in the delivery, but without a strong rationale it is merely a method of arrogantly disarming an opponent. A strong argument should be convincing because it is plausible and built on evidence.

Kuhn and Udell (2007, p. 90) suggest that argumentation in academia is 'The dialogic process in which two or more people engage in debate of opposing claims.' Such a debate requires substantiation, and each argument is subject to scrutiny by knowledgeable others. An academic argument, then, can often be a claim to knowledge – a persuasive statement designed to convince the listener that the claims made are robust and worthwhile. Such an argument should emanate from a foundation of knowing, and in order to build a strong case for your argument, it is useful to explore some of the elements of argumentation itself. This can enable you to become a better scholar because it deepens your understanding of phenomena. In support of this, Lapakko (2021, p. 3) suggests that to understand how an argument works we should explore 'the nature of claims, the evidence that supports them, and the assumptions behind each point.'

To see this in practice, let's suppose you are yet to locate your evidence but are following a premise that you feel is a strong one. You believe that all the members of a particular profession are overworked and are thus looking to leave as soon as possible. You may have even heard somewhere that there is a shortage in this area and it is because of working conditions. But where does that thinking originate? Social media? Friends? From the profession itself? Your investigation reveals that the initial assumption is wrong and that the vast majority of professionals in that field consistently find their careers to be both exciting and rewarding. But this is why research is conducted and is why we need to follow the evidence. The picture is often far more complex than we imagine, and having that evidence gives your argument credence.

To exemplify how an argument can be generated, we can draw on the field of English and a fundamental approach to the critical reading of a text. If you studied English, you may be familiar with something called *Point, Evidence, Explain* (and its unfortunate acronym). If not, it does not matter as it is a simple premise. Point, Evidence, Explain (PEE) requires you to make a point (present an argument), provide evidence to validate your point, then expand on this evidence to explain the potential complexity. It is a basic approach but useful to get you started if you have been out of studying for some time. And you can develop the intricacy of your argument as you progress. To use PEE, let's suppose your reading illustrates that the policies around equality and diversity in engineering are outdated and lacking in awareness of recent societal changes. You can make your claim and draw on your evidence to support it (Kuhn, 1999). The next step is to analyse your evidence and use it to provide depth to your claim, thus strengthening your rationale for why the claim is valid (Hahn et al., 2009). To do this,

TABLE 7.1 Point, evidence, explain

Point	Evidence*	Explain
Profession is dwindling	Numerous studies argue for the counter argument (e.g. Abbott, 2021; Smith, 2024; Woodward, 2022).	The profession is expanding and becoming more attractive for graduates. However, professional status is dwindling.
Professional skills do not align with employers	Zhabi (2023)	Professional standards need updating as they are no longer fit for purpose.
Public perception is flawed	Brown (2023), Cackler (2023), and Zhang (2024)	Numerous memes on social media are providing disinformation. Professional representation is no longer available through the profession's awarding body.

*NB. Fictitious references used solely for exemplary purposes.

you might decide to collate your findings in tabular form and Table 7.1 illustrates what this could look like.

▶ ROBUST PRACTICES

Many undergraduate errors in academic arguments arise from sloppy practices regarding evidence – loose claims that are assumed to be true because they are either rumoured that way or the individual feels that to be the case. Or claims that 'there is no literature on this area' when in reality the student clearly has not looked as there is actually an abundance of it. If there is evidence out there, seek it out and use it to your advantage. Evidence is not only useful for backing up your claims, it can also dispute what you believe as you need to have an open approach to knowledge construction. Even experienced researchers should minimise bias where possible and suppress personal beliefs that are unsubstantiated. Many apparently well-thought-through hypotheses fail to play out in practice because the evidence contradicts the expectations.

You will recall from earlier chapters that the academic literature we draw on as a body of evidence for a particular field of study was analogised to a large and ongoing academic conversation. However, unlike the online debates between political opponents, each research article, book or book chapter attempts to present a robust case through the (sometimes tacit) ethical procedure it has followed and the rigorous methodology it has applied. And, through peer review and publication, a small team of experts in the field have validated the process. Arguing your point in writing is similar as you will be subject to scrutiny. It is necessary, then, for it to stand up to this scrutiny and knowing the details of your argument will enable you to achieve this. Whilst in a debate you are unlikely to be expected to cite your sources, it is in your best interest to at least be familiar with the literature. This gives you the confidence to speak out on the matter and it is your way of showing that you really know your stuff. In writing, this is necessary and in order to prove your point, and to argue it robustly, you need supporting literature. In this way, you demonstrate how it is substantiated and, if possible, instantiated. This means that you present your argument, you show the evidence for it (substantiation) and if applicable you identify where this occurs or how it applies (instantiation). This paves the way for a really strong argument. You have situated it within the existing understanding and thus have evidence to prove that what you are saying represents the current state of the field.

Types of evidence

As mentioned above, the evidence you need to support your argument is that which is deemed to be both robust and reliable. But there is a myriad of sources out there and getting to know which ones are acceptable and which ones are not can be extremely tricky (see also 'sourcing your literature' in Chapter 6). Let's start off with discarding some of the more useless ones as this is much easier. For your studies in engineering, you have been given a task on identifying and evaluating nature's materials. What are they and how effective are they? What purpose could they be used for? You decide to place your luck in an internet search and eventually find some websites that are accessible and appear useful. This is not academic enquiry, however, and you probably do not know the value of these sources. Who has posted this information? What is their bias? How can I accept this as factual? The types of evidence you are looking for should be representative of the knowledge of the field – in this instance, academic journals related to engineering. These will be identified by your course tutors and there is a good chance that if the university library subscribes to them they will be reliable. Your course tutors will recommend journals to the library and will be able to advise on any that are not worth subscribing to. This is a good start and you can revisit Chapter 6 for more information. I will finish on Google Scholar, however, as that can be useful too.

Google Scholar is improving daily and captures a wide range of studies. The disadvantage of this is that because of publishers' paywalls, they are not always available to access. However, your university library can probably handle an inter-library loan. You will also need to know how to validate your sources as the quality of publications can vary enormously. Academic publishing is a highly complex area, and differentiating between vanity publishers and reputable journals can require a great deal of experience. As there is not enough room to fully discuss it here, then, I would make two suggestions to start you off:

1) Use your reading lists as a guide to which journals are valid.
2) Speak to an academic, perhaps your personal tutor, for advice.

Worldviews – know your standpoint

Our worldview, or standpoint on life, is how we see everything around us, and exploring it can lead to deep and philosophical reflection. It involves what we think knowledge is (ontology) and how we believe it is created (epistemology). But it often shapes the arguments we make, the ideologies we buy into, and the political beliefs we have. From the perspective of constructing an argument, it is useful to understand your worldview because it is influential on how you position yourself within an argument

(Sadler et al., 2004). This means that you will naturally hold some kind of bias in the way you see the world. This is fine, this is the norm, but understanding it – as well as the standpoints of others – helps you to strengthen your argument and to separate the facts from your beliefs, each of which may influence your opinion.

For instance, you may hold the opinion that higher education (HE) should be free to everyone. Or perhaps a friend suggests that HE is a level of education that not everybody needs, and that taxpayers' money could be spent in more productive ways. In which case, your friend would agree with the fees students are charged for their education. These are opinions but they are shaped by your standpoint. This is part of who you are and it sometimes steers how you frame your argument. Being aware of your worldview is important because you will need to understand the worldview of others and thus avoid the blinkered approach. This enables you to point out the flaws in your own argument and thus dissuades you from mere superficial engagement as you become aware of the potential depth of your argument.

Know your argument

It may sound silly to say that you should know your own argument but there are many people who argue, protest, demonstrate, and complain vociferously about an issue they know little about. Some have engaged in social media and have been misinformed, whilst others are merely imitating someone they admire and reproducing their arguments. Statements, beliefs and opinions are subject to replication and development as they can undergo memetic transfer (Tindale, 2017). That is, they change in nature, and this results in many people buying into an idea or an ideology that they do not fully understand. It has even been known for some people to have engaged fully with an issue – gone on a demonstration, for instance – without understanding the full rationale for why they are there. This is dangerous and can fuel division. And why would you wish to support something that you do not fully buy into? This is not to say that you should not demonstrate, of course. Demonstrating is a valid form of protesting for a worthwhile concern. But how well you understand the justification for this, and how informed are you to make a judgement that it is the correct thing to do, is really worth considering.

Informed protestors are in a more powerful position as they are fully aware of the issue they are standing against and why it is important to make this stand. To draw on an interesting analogy here (particularly useful if you are studying drama or performing arts), an actor needs to know her/his part incredibly well. This is more than merely learning the lines that the character will speak, however. Let's use Cynthia as an example. Cynthia is performing Lady Macbeth in *Macbeth* at the West End (London). Cynthia is a method actor and really aims to get beneath the fingernails of her characters. That is, she wants to understand how they function and what motivates them in every way. This goes beyond understanding one's motivation for moving around the stage, it is the character's innermost thoughts, desires, and behaviours; in fact, it is their life beyond the stage. Cynthia asks herself questions such as what time does Lady Macbeth get out of bed? What does she eat for breakfast? How does she spend her day? In this way, Cynthia grows to understand Lady Macbeth (or at least her interpretation of her) in a deep and meaningful way. Cynthia is also confident that she can engage in a 'hotseat' activity where random questions are fired at her in character – e.g. who was your mother? What was the profession of your father? Who is your closest friend? Cynthia is thus ready to metaphorically live and breathe her Lady Macbeth persona.

You obviously do not need to go to this level of detail with your argument, but hopefully you get the idea of what it means to have a strong case. As a mature student, you dip into the world of academia as a student but should try to understand it through the eyes of an academic. If you know the field, are cognisant of the key arguments, you will be able to defend your own argument. We know our argument well, by understanding the background to it and the rationale for why it is the best stance to take in light of other options. It is thus important to explore the strengths of the counter arguments. What is the key argument that a potential opponent to you would propose? What is it that they have that could poke holes in your argument? Do you need to revise your thinking? Is your own argument flawed? Knowing the counter argument well enables you to challenge it more.

Understand the counter argument

In the current political climate there seems to be a strong, and highly politicised, drive to outdo one's opponents. Many accusations are thrown wildly against opposing political voices, and concepts such as 'cancel culture' and 'woke' have entered the language. Some claim that cancel culture is a fictitious concept, devised by the political right as a riposte to the necessary censoring of harmful words or actions towards others. Others, however, argue that cancel culture is a tool of the political left and is a means of culling the opposition, of closing down important conversations, and of ensuring that only one ideology prevails. Whilst these are often seen as the political left versus the political right, that is not always as the case, and applying such a straightforward binary model as this fails to capture the complexity of the conflict. There are opposing forces in action and the overlap is far from straightforward, which means you have to unpick the arguments and explore the details. This is a useful example of how arguments often work as it illustrates flaws and potential biases, such as political perspectives. If you can temporarily position yourself neutrally, you can see this in action in debates (perhaps online). Try to avoid the content and taking a particular side but be honest with yourself and note who makes the stronger argument and why. Was it the conviction with which the speaker presented it? What evidence was used? Why does the counter argument appear weaker? With practice, you can actually disagree with someone yet still evaluate the strength of their argument in a neutral manner.

Stay true to form

There are many shenanigans used in professional debates so it is useful to know (but not use) these if you are interested in the mechanics of argumentation. For instance, in a typical debate that you can easily find online, you will be able to witness a variety of sharp and misleading practices, from using and abusing statistics, adopting a 'straw man' (person?) argument, switching the focus to meet the strengths of the speaker, to deliberate misinterpretations or downright lying. This is not something you should wish to adopt for yourself, however. But identifying these factors in others will help you to further strengthen your own position. It will also enable you to evaluate an argument more objectively. For instance, it is very useful to know when someone is using a straw man argument because if unnoticed it can draw you in to defending something you are not actually arguing for. Or it can position you in an unfair way, even resulting in you being erroneously 'labelled.' You then exert a lot of energy in defending yourself rather than dismissing the strategy altogether. This is a form of discourse entrapment, leaving you trying to get out of a hole that was actually dug by your opponent. Let's look at some examples of these to see how ideas can become accepted and how you can identify a flawed argument. First, the straw man argument which is used as a counter argument.

Speaker A: The problem we have today is poor awareness in young people of the dangers of unprotected sex. I think that the school is the proper place to educate them on this.

Speaker B: You can't just encourage young people to become sexually active. That's not the way forward.

You will see from this that Speaker A's intention has been misinterpreted and that s/he is now being accused of the very thing that s/he is arguing against. The strawman argument is flawed in that it does not actually refute the argument that has been presented; rather, it presents it as another argument, one that is much easier to disprove. This can be an extremely powerful way of dominating the conversation. The discussion here is on how, where and when young people should learn about sex. But Speaker A is explicitly accused of promoting sexual activism in young people. If Speaker A takes the bait, s/he might adopt a defensive position on this and this weakens her/him. This would subsequently empower Speaker

B, but it is a disingenuous accusation and possibly a deliberate misinterpretation of Speaker A's words. This might mask the fact that Speaker B does not have a strong alternative argument. Making someone else's argument look weak in order to gain the upper hand is a simplistic yet devious strategy. Rather than identifying the weaknesses in the argument, it fabricates some and attacks those. And unfortunately this often works because the audience can miss the switch and become swept along with the supposed counter argument.

If successful, the straw man argument positions and categorises an opponent in a particular way and this is also done with labelling. For example, 'you have radical ideas' or 'you are a bigot.' Once that label sticks, the opponent gains the upper hand, and the speaker loses credibility. Whatever the speaker says after this is often dismissed by the audience as the trust has been lost. Speaker A can respond to the straw man argument in a variety of ways. S/he can provide a defence for this or a denial, restating their case clearly and hoping to be heard/understood. They can identify and mentally note the trick that was used, dismissing it and moving onto firmer terrain (talking about what they know). They could (politely) correct the supposed misinterpretation and reemphasize their point. Or, they could explicitly point it out as a manipulative action that the opponent took and thus disarm the user.

If Speaker A uses the first approach, as many people do when unprepared or unaware of what has happened, they may appear guilty. This is a defensive manoeuvre and makes Speaker A look like s/he is backtracking. Of course, a straw man argument can sometimes arise from a genuine misinterpretation. However, more often than not it is an intentionally manipulative strategy aimed at shifting the balance of power, particularly if the user either has a weak argument or is losing the debate. After all, if you had a really strong argument, wouldn't you be best positioned in just presenting it? Whilst it is useful to understand how argumentation is used (and abused), you should think ethically about your own position and avoid using the straw man argument yourself. Rather, you should call it out for what it is. It is disingenuous and experienced speakers (and listeners) will see it immediately.

Constructing an Argument   103

Position yourself as the experienced speaker, then, and it will be the user of the straw man that will actually lose credibility.

Here is another one:

Speaker C: Prisons are full and the prison system needs to be revamped so that it fully rehabilitates its offenders. It would be better if we took prisoners who are coming towards the end of their sentences and placed them on a bespoke programme of rehabilitation.

Speaker D: So you think we should just let all the paedophiles and murderers out early? That's the cure for society, is it – endanger the general public even more by giving prisoners shorter sentences?

Hopefully it is clear that Speaker D is manipulating the conversation and misrepresenting Speaker C's words. When you watch an online debate and see evidence of this, then, note what the other speaker does and what the reaction is from the chair and audience.

Another strategy you may see, particularly in political debates, is where a speaker shifts the conversation onto what they want to talk about because that positions them in a stronger way. It is also used to avoid difficult questions. Here is an example:

Reporter: Whilst you have been in power the unemployment figure has increased significantly. Can you explain this?

Politician: We have put hundreds of thousands of pounds into our Careers for Everyone initiative over the last two years. We have provided opportunities for many individuals to fully utilise their education in a manner that is most suitable for them, and clearly matches their aspirations. It is important for young people to wake up in the morning and to have a clear and meaningful sense of purpose in life. We are creating that purpose by incentivising children and young

> people in schools and colleges and guiding them onto successful career paths. We believe that a career should speak to the heart of the individual and should resonate with their ambitions to succeed. A career is more than just a job, it is part of who we are. So we feel that it is important to get this right from the outset.

What was the question again? As you can see, the response runs on and carries little meaning in relation to the question that was actually posed. It certainly does not answer it. The politician steers the conversation onto solid ground where s/he can speak fluently on matters that s/he is familiar with. It's the subtle equivalent of saying, 'I don't want to talk about that, I want to talk about this instead,' but it puts the politician in control. The politician relays what s/he has rehearsed and draws on material s/he is confident with. In many ways this is a hidden agenda, where the politician has something that they want to say and just needs to find a place to deliver it. Whatever the conversation, then, s/he will shift the focus so that s/he can talk about what s/he had planned

Once you are aware of this and look out for it, you will find that conversations are very interesting and informative in ways that perhaps they shouldn't be. They tell you a lot about the speaker and, if we choose to listen, we can hear a lot about what the speaker wants to tells us. Many experienced speakers engage in this type of activity because it empowers them and it wins people over. Why? Because the average person does not listen intensely or with a critical ear. This does not mean that they are not intelligent, of course. Rather, they are merely listening to what is being said and how that resonates with their own lives; they are not necessarily looking out for manipulative strategies. And as with the straw man examples above, if they agree with what has been said they are less likely to question its relevance in the conversation.

The majority of people listening to a debate don't analyse what was said unless they are suspicious or somehow have a vested interest. This is why conversational tactics such as these are persuasive. They tap into an emotional connection that we have with our fellow humans. In the reporter-politician example above, we may get wrapped up in positive thoughts of young people waking up in the morning and feeling inspired. We may even think, 'yes, that is a compassionate person who is merely trying to do what is in everyone's best interest.' But what we are not seeing, or perhaps choosing to ignore because our emotions override this, is the manipulation and the evasive tactics the politician employs. And reporters often get swept along with this as the person weasels out of answering the question, or just give up as they feel there is little point pursuing it. However, some do not accept this and push their interviewees for a response, as can be seen in the Jeremy Paxman interview of Home Secretary Michael Howard on 13th May 1997. You can easily find this online and if you do choose to view it, look out for the 'Did you threaten to overrule him?' question and watch carefully how Howard handles this. This is a persuasive technique used to bring the conversation back to something that the speaker is comfortable with. Politicians are great at doing this because they have a narrative that they need to sell and do their utmost to shift the conversation onto this.

As an argumentative strategy, this technique does have its strengths as long as it is used ethically. Using it to avoid someone's questions or to close them down is poor practice. However, on those occasions when an opponent is trying to do just that to you, or is aiming to linguistically trip you up, shifting the focus onto what you are confident with can redress the imbalance. In general, this is a strategy that you should perhaps use sparingly but be fully aware of when engaged in debates. If you do not realise what the other party is doing when they are being evasive like this it can be disconcerting and cause you to doubt yourself.

▶ CONCLUSION

In academia, executing a strong argument involves the presentation of evidence (Kuhn, 1999), much of which is available in the literature of the field you are studying. Knowing this field helps you to position your argument well and strengthens its essential constituents. In constructing an argument, it is also useful to understand how the process of argumentation itself occurs, and this chapter explored a variety of strategies used by debaters and professional speakers. Whilst some provide an effective foundation upon which you can build a robust argument, others are merely aimed at raising awareness of the manipulative and disingenuous approaches that some employ. Seeing how argumentation can work in this way, then, can enable you to not only identify poor practice but to remain ethical in your own approach, gathering evidence and presenting it openly. In the next chapter we shall examine the key components of academic writing, enabling you to present your argument both explicitly and succinctly in written form.

▶ REFERENCES

Epstein, R. L. (2018). *The fundamentals of argument analysis: Essays on logic as the art of reasoning well*. Advanced Reasoning Forum.

Hahn, U., Harris, A. J. L., & Corner, A. (2009). Argument content and argument source: An exploration. *Informal Logic*, *29*(4), 337. https://doi.org/10.22329/il.v29i4.2903

Kuhn, D. (1999). *The skills of argument*. Cambridge University Press.

Kuhn, D., & Udell, W. (2007). Coordinating own and other perspectives in argument. *Thinking & Reasoning*, *13*(2), 90–104. https://doi.org/10.1080/13546780600625447

Lapakko, D. (2021). *Argumentation: Critical thinking in action*. 5th ed. Kendall Hunt Publishing Company.

Merriam-Webster. (2024, March 11). *Definition of "argument"*. www.merriam-Webster.com. https://www.merriam-webster.com/dictionary/argument#:~:text=%3A%20a%20reason%20for%20or%20against

Sadler, T. D., Chambers, F. W., & Zeidler, D. L. (2004). Student conceptualizations of the nature of science in response to a socioscientific issue. *International Journal of Science Education*, *26*(4), 387–409. https://doi.org/10.1080/0950069032000119456

Tindale, C. W. (2017). Replicating reasons: Arguments, memes, and the cognitive environment. *Philosophy & Rhetoric*, *50*(4), 566–588. https://doi.org/10.5325/philrhet.50.4.0566

8 Academic Writing

▶ INTRODUCTION

Writing is a method of articulating ideas and thoughts, and in many ways it is an alternative to orally presenting ideas. But many people who can articulate their ideas clearly, often expressing profound thoughts with impressive linguistic ability, struggle to do so in written form. These people are often great theorisers and can grapple with concepts in the same way that academics grapple with concepts, theories, and frameworks for understanding in their writing. But they do so verbally and the written word intimidates them. This is a position that many mature students find themselves in, having been out of education for some time (Kahu et al., 2014). Of course, academic writing is a different skill from speaking. It requires a structured approach to the presentation of words and the use of language that can not only demonstrate complex ideas, but also adhere to the rules. But I would argue that both speaking and writing can be very close in nature. Whilst academic writing is more than just putting your thoughts on paper, if you can articulate complex thoughts verbally then you are well on your way to transferring these into academic writing. Moreover, you can utilise the nature of writing itself as it allows you to craft and recraft your words – honing them so they are succinct and the meaning is explicit. Spoken words cannot be retrieved but writing can be polished until it is ready to be released into the public domain. As such, you can rework your writing so that it explores and explains complex matters in detailed and accessible ways.

Academic writing and the ability to express oneself intellectually both share a common foundation, that of grappling with complex concepts and relaying them to an audience. For many, making the change is based on confidence, experience, and perhaps some seemingly problematic use of grammar. We will not look at addressing grammar needs here, however, as that is something you can explore yourself online and which your university may also offer. Rather, the focus of this chapter is on melding the two forms of communication to enable you as a mature student to write more confidently. It is hoped that this chapter will enable you to recognise your existing ability to express ideas and subsequently encourage you to channel these through a different medium – that of the convention of academic writing.

▶ THE LITERATURE LEADS THE WAY

Good writing is based on effective reading, and you should have a strong knowledge of the literature before you write. This is not to say that you cannot record your ideas, of course, or note down points you would like to write about. In fact, you may wish to plan your writing by identifying the key points of your argument and some themes you would like to explore. But if you find yourself engaged in uninformed free writing – writing from the heart rather than building on existing understanding – you are likely to include bias, employ conjecture, and pose many unsubstantiated claims. This is because you are drawing on your memory (as well as being influenced by your ideology) and this is not a reliable approach, particularly when we know that memories can be highly flawed (Shaw, 2017). Your argument is important, of course, but it must be shaped by your engagement with current thinking in your field. Academic investigation relies on interacting with a body of literature (i.e. where existing understanding is housed) and seeks to build on this knowledge.

When you use the literature to lead your argument, it strengthens it significantly. Firstly, it promotes robustness because it is based on previously validated arguments. And secondly, it actually makes the writing easier for you – the ideas are there you just need to draw them out. If you are not familiar with the literature, you rely on your own resources and draw on your creativity to manufacture ideas and propositions. That makes for a great for a piece of creative writing, of course, but it cannot be validated as an academic argument. A much stronger approach is to understand the field and then draw on your creativity to develop it. This requires you to synthesize ideas, build connections, and perhaps generate an innovative approach to examining the field. Combining knowledge and creativity is arguably a force to be reckoned with.

Using the literature in this way is superior to uninformed freewriting because we generally write about what we know. In freewriting, we write about what we think we know but if we have not sought the evidence in the first place we are in an academically weak position. A common mistake for some undergraduates is to begin with the freewriting approach, with typical reasons for doing so acting as poor justifications:

> I knew about this topic because it's been in the media a lot.
> It looked easy.

Aside from the academic weakness of this approach, it can also be much harder to do. Those individuals who begin this way are often under the impression that a citation or two bolted on the end of some of the sentences can signify academic engagement. However, this approach is usually evident in the writing, with citations seemingly out of place and it is sometimes unclear what they are referring to. Moreover, some even go to great lengths to find a source to raise the academic appearance of their work but, not having read the text, fail to realise that the source does not actually support what they are claiming.

As tempting as this approach might be when you are pushed for time or cannot face the idea of reading all those articles, you really

TABLE 8.1 Writing approaches

Reason	Explanation
Your argument may be flawed	That does not work with what we currently know.
Your argument may be biased	That is not the case for many people.
You have misunderstood the article	That is not what the author said.
Your idea is weak	That concept has been debunked widely in the literature.
Your source is old	A lot has been written since then (including newer publications by that author)
Your source is invalid	That author has been contested and thinking has moved on significantly.
You are not engaging with your sources	The authors say a lot more than that and you should elaborate on your points.

are doing yourself a disservice. From experience, I can tell you that many students who have worked on an assignment in this way have later realised that it is in fact harder and have willingly changed to a literature-led approach. To convince you further, Table 8.1 provides a brief list of some of the reasons why you should not merely engage in uninformed freewriting for your assignments.

There are many more reasons why you should use the literature to inform your argument but hopefully you will be convinced at this stage so let's move on to structure.

▶ STRUCTURE

Academic writing is usually assessed through the submission of assignments and these need to be structured with a coherent and logical narrative. As a general rule, you would typically have some form of introduction, the central body of the argument, and then a conclusion. There is an old adage, attributed by some to Aristotle, that is often applied to speeches and formally written arguments/ essays. It goes something like this:

> Tell them what you're going to tell them; tell them; then, tell them what you told them.

Of course, you need to build the detail and complexity of your argument beyond this, but it is a useful starting point for your structure. It has the essence of what you need and illustrates the direction of travel for your narrative. Let's look at an example question to see how this works in practice:

> Write an essay on the conventions of studying for a degree online versus attending a university in person.

Tell them what you're going to tell them

You begin by explaining the purpose of the essay. There may be some signposting in this section, but it is not necessary to reveal your findings or central argument at this stage. This phase sets the scene and gives the reader an indication of the overall content. It includes your introduction and might provide some context for understanding the argument. In general, this section prepares your reader for what is to come. For the example, you might talk about learning in general and independent study as an essential part of HE, before giving a definition of what you mean by online learning: 'correspondence courses' or 'distance education' as opposed to your university running a Teams session one week because a lecturer needs to be off site. If your essay favours one form over the other, this information might not appear here but could be withheld until later. You might, however, allude to the fact that you found one to be stronger than the other and will therefore discuss this further in the main body. This is sort of a teaser and there is a balance to get right here between providing enough information to make the reader interested, and want to read on, and giving too much information so that the reader feels hereon nothing new will be added.

Tell them

This is the main body of your argument and it might be split into subsections, such as themes under subheadings. This is the section in which you will unpick the central arguments, analysing the details and evaluating the two forms of learning. You might choose to take each one separately, presenting the case and critiquing it, or you may decide to evaluate them together under headings, such as Potential for Engagement, Opportunities for Collaboration, *Classroom Learning, Dealing with Enquiries, The Student Perspective, Learning Strategies* and so on. You would end this section by demonstrating a strong and substantiated argument and reveal your hand. This is likely to be the longest section.

Tell them what you told them

This is the section where you reiterate the main points and demonstrate the significance of the essay. You are not necessarily just repeating what you have said, however; you are merely summarizing it for a 'take away message.' Furthermore, a good conclusion looks to the future – what further research might be needed, what are the limitations of your argument or factors that could not be considered but might play a role in a larger investigation, and so on. Our assignment for this example, then, might look a little something like this when it is finished:

- **Introduction**
  - *Identify approach*
  - *Present comparison*
  - *Outline history*
  - *Define forms*
- **Online learning**
  - *Pros and cons*
- **Attending a university in person**
  - *Pros and cons*
- **Findings**
  - *Central argument*
  - *Limitations*

- **Conclusion**
  - *Where do we go from here?*

Having a structure such as this will not only help get you started, it will keep you on track as you write. You should avoid being overly descriptive, however, in favour of being analytical. That is, avoid telling the reader what is going on but explain why. Whilst you might have information to provide (description), you can still be critical with how you present it, i.e. explore the underlying elements and unpack it.

You may be given a template for your assignment but devising your own structure is a useful exercise for ensuring you have a firm overview of your response. There are mixed views on the strengths of templates. Some argue that as you are doing a degree you should be more independent and design your own. Others feel that a template is merely a guide and how you engage with the question is more important. Either way it is worth trying to understand the rationale for your structure. A template can be useful but it is only as good as the person who understands it and can use it. It can be difficult to fit your writing into one if you have strong ideas on how you would like to shape it. If in doubt, speak to your tutor for advice. Whatever structure you choose, it is essential that you address the question and meet the learning outcomes.

Perhaps the most effective way to understand a structure is to see it in action, and I would strongly recommend that you have a look at some existing essays (ones by established writers should provide good examples) and analyse the structures. Look for the three parts we discuss above and see what else you can identify. Have the authors used this approach? Is it more complex? If so, how? And why? What is the effect of the layout the authors have used? You can also ask yourself questions such as when are the findings or central arguments presented? How are they presented? How robust are the claims and what supporting evidence is given? And finally, what assumptions are made on the audience? This is a factor you will need to consider. Are you writing for a novice audience? Your lecturer may know the field well but s/he will probably still expect you to not take your reader for granted.

Models of argumentation

Another way to structure your essay could be to draw on the Toulmin model of argumentation, introduced in 1958 (Toulmin et al., 1979). This is a straightforward model and thus appealing for mature students who have been out of formal learning for over a year. The model proposes a six-step process: Claim; Grounds; Warrant; Backing; Rebuttal; Qualifier. First you make your claim or argument. Then you ground that claim in evidence. And then you show how the evidence warrants the claim. Karbach (1987) suggests that the first three steps of the process are present in all arguments, so the latter three are not essential. These further steps are used to support the first three, as can be seen by the following explanation:

> The qualifier, when present, is sometimes used in the wording of the claim and is therefore different from the rebuttal and backing which are only implied. The backing establishes the reliability and relevance of the warrant; the rebuttal acknowledges exceptions that might invalidate the claim; and, the qualifier modifies the claim.
>
> (Karbach, 1987, p. 82)

This is a model that you could use to present an argument when exploring your themes in the main body of your writing. The simplicity of the Toulmin model, particularly if you only employ the first three elements, is its strength as it can be quickly and smoothly applied. And it is also effective for counterarguments, wherein you present and dismantle those arguments that purport to challenge yours. If models of argumentation such as this interest you, there are many other ones that you might wish to explore, such as the Rogerian theory (Young et al., 1970), or Andrews (Andrews, 2005).

▶ TO QUOTE, OR NOT TO QUOTE

Once you have your structure in place, you will need to think about how you use the literature. As mentioned throughout this book, when undertaking a degree you are expected to read widely and engage with the key texts. Reading constitutes your scholarly activity and enables you to become knowledgeable in your field. Your reading is captured in your notetaking (see Chapter 5) and includes the ideas and arguments you have gleaned from the literature. Anything that is used to inform your writing will need to be acknowledged and there are various ways you can do this. You can include a direct quote (the author's words) verbatim or in an abridged form, providing you do not alter the meaning. Or you can paraphrase the words, putting them into your own construction. The examples below explore how this can be tackled, and the layout of in-text referencing is also discussed in Chapter 9. Here are two ways in which you might handle the same information:

> Between 2015 and 2020, questions were raised by key figures in relation to the effectiveness of the company's health and safety policy.
>
> (Bingley & Bhagat, 2023)

According to Bingley & Bhagat (2023, p. 145),

> In the five-year period preceding the Covid-19 outbreak, ministers asked the following three questions on the institution's health and safety policy: 1) Why hasn't this policy been updated in two years? 2) Who is currently in charge of quality assurance? 3) Is this policy fit for purpose?

In the first example, the author paraphrases and cites Bingley & Bhagat (2023) to acknowledge where the evidence for this statement came from. In the second one, the author allows Bingley & Bhagat to state the case in their own words. Essentially, there is no difference in meaning. However, the second is more detailed and direct quotes have the upper hand in relation to accuracy – paraphrasing can lead to misinterpretation. But this does not mean that the second is stronger in academic terms. In fact, you might decide that it is actually weaker in that it gives more information than is needed and could suggest editorial laziness on the author's behalf. You may wonder, then, when it is appropriate to use the author's words and when it is more suitable for you to paraphrase them. If you wish to present a more succinct version of what the author is saying, you might choose to represent the ideas in your own words. As a rule of thumb, however, but by no means an idea set in stone, you should include the author's words if you feel that you could not represent something yourself as effectively and succinctly as the author has done. In other words, if the author says it better than you could why change it? Consider, for instance, the following examples:

> **Author 1**
> In Act 3, scene 1, Hamlet questions the turmoil of life and asks whether it is better to exist or not to exist. Is it better and more noble to tolerate life's torments and the problems we face, he asks, or should one challenge the torment by not accepting it and choosing death? Is death just one long sleep in which we are no longer tormented? Perhaps there's something in that after all, Hamlet concludes. When we die, we sleep.
>
> **Author 2**
> In Act 3, Scene 1, Hamlet (Shakespeare, 1623) reflects on the vagaries of life and philosophises about humanity and our very existence:
>
>> *"To be, or not to be", that is the question:*
>> *Whether 'tis Nobler in the minde to suffer*
>> *The Slings and Arrowes of outrageous Fortune;*
>> *Or to take Armes against a Sea of troubles,*
>> *And, by opposing, end them: to dye, to sleepe–*
>> *No more – and, by a sleepe, to say we end*
>> *The Heart-ake, and the thousand Naturall shockes*
>> *That Flesh is heyre too? 'Tis a consummation*
>> *Deuoutly to be wish'd. To dye to sleepe.*

The second author is not attempting to go head-to-head with Shakespeare and feels that paraphrasing in this instance would commit a disservice to the author as it would fail to capture the vivid evocation and beautiful imagery of the soliloquy. And, of course, an interpretation would not be without its critics. As Wilson (2017, p. 341) suggests, the classic line of *To be, or not to be* 'is probably the most famous line in the most famous passage in the most famous play by the most famous artist in Western history.'

▶ PHRASING YOUR THOUGHTS

As argued earlier, the ability to verbally express a complex idea is in many ways similar to portraying this in written form. The difference perhaps lies in the formatting and the revising of what has been said to fit the mould of academic writing. This requires an understanding of the way academic writing is presented, and one of the most effective ways to improve your academic writing is to read academic papers. In doing so, you not only assimilate ideas and arguments, you also adopt language use in your own writing. Indeed, many successful writers themselves mimic the style of those they admire. For more practical help for actual language, however, you may be interested in Academic Phrasebank, developed by the University of Manchester. Here is an example comprising various statements that can be used when referencing 'literature to justify a method or approach' (University of Manchester, 2023, p. 48):

> In a recent article, Smith (2009) argues that case studies offer …
> Smith et al. (1994) identify several advantages of the case study …
> Jones (2012) argues that case studies are useful when the conditions of the research …
> According to Smith (2011), semi-structured interviews have a wide-spread popularity in …

As you can see, numerous examples are given of how you might present an argument for using a particular research method. This is a useful resource as it can help you mould the language you use to fit the academic style. To sum up, then, the following points are recommended for writing an assignment:

- **Read widely** – This influences how you write and the language you use. Reading in your field will help you to identify the particular style of writing that is favoured as academic writing is a broad term and varies widely across disciplines.
- **Devise a structure** – Set the scene, add in context, present your argument critically, demonstrate resolution and ways forward
- **Avoid uninformed free writing** but use the literature to lead your argument
- **Begin writing early** – After reading, get your thoughts down on paper (Word doc), regardless of the shape they are in. This builds confidence and you can revise the language later to suit the academic style.
- **Establish a strong overall coherence to your argument** – Does the narrative flow, sequentially? Does the order make sense in relation to your key argument?
- **Revisit the learning outcomes to ensure you meet them**

In the next chapter, we will continue our quest with academic writing by exploring the purpose of referencing and how you can make the most of this in your work.

▶ REFERENCES

Andrews, R. (2005). Models of argumentation in educational discourse. *Text – Interdisciplinary Journal for the Study of Discourse*, 25(1). https://doi.org/10.1515/text.2005.25.1.107

Bingley & Bhagat. (2023). *Fictitious reference used to exemplify paraphrasing*.

Kahu, E., Stephens, C., Leach, L., & Zepke, N. (2014). Linking academic emotions and student engagement: Mature-aged distance students' transition to university. *Journal of Further and Higher Education*, 39(4), 481–497. https://doi.org/10.1080/0309877x.2014.895305

Karbach, J. (1987). Using Toulmin's model of argumentation. *Journal of Teaching Writing*, 6(1), 81–91.

Shakespeare, W. (2009). *The works of Shakespeare: tragedies* (1st ed.). Geddes & Grosset.

Shaw, J. (2017). *The memory illusion: Why you might not be who you think you are.* Anchor Canada.

Toulmin, S. E., Rieke, R. D., & Janik, A. (1979). *An introduction to reasoning.* Macmillan.

University of Manchester. (2023). Academic phrasebank. Academic Phrasebank. https://www.phrasebank.manchester.ac.uk/

Wilson, J. R. (2017). "To be, or not to be": Shakespeare against philosophy. *Shakespeare, 14*(4), 341–359. https://doi.org/10.1080/17450918.2017.1343376

Young, R. E., Becker, A. L., & Pike, K. L. (1970). *Rhetoric: Discovery and change.* Hartcourt, Brace & World.

9 Referencing

▶ WHAT IS REFERENCING AND WHY DO WE NEED IT?

The Cambridge Dictionary (2024 online) defines one use of the term 'reference' as 'a mention of something,' and in general we use the term 'refer' to draw someone's attention to something, often steering that person towards further details. For instance, we might reference a friend in a conversation (speak about them) or give reference to a particular place. This can be to identify the friend or the location or it might be to include more information on them. Referencing that denotes some form of signposting to an item or place provides an analogous use of the way the word is employed in an academic context. Indeed, the academic convention of referencing involves signposting the reader to the source of supporting evidence. Referencing is an academic skill and as a student it is important for you to understand the mechanics of it, as well as the rationale for why you are doing it. An academic reference is a mention of the location or origin of the supporting evidence and thus provides a trail for the recipient to follow. This trail can be pursued by understanding the academic conventions of referencing, such as that provided in a typical reference list or bibliography. These provide fuller details for you as a student to

DOI: 10.4324/9781032619255-9

follow up. Look at the following book reference to see how this plays out:

Cain, T. [Ed.] (2018) *Becoming a research-informed school: Why? what? how?* London: Routledge. ISBN 9781138308640.

We begin understanding the reference (reading from the left) with the author or editor. The example used is a book that looks at how research can be utilised and conducted in schools. The name 'Cain' is the surname of the key person attributed to the book, and 'T' is the initial of his first name: 'Timothy'. The 'Ed' in square brackets denotes that the key person is not an author of the whole book (although there are large sections in this particular book authored by Cain) but is in fact the editor. This means that he is the person responsible for compiling all the chapters and overseeing the process of putting the book together. You will see lots of variations to this format, such as the full use of the first name, the year of publication appearing elsewhere, words being abridged, and the omission of the ISBN, and some of these will be discussed later. Books such as this are multi-authored and this can be seen in the contents list, where each chapter is listed with a byline (name of the person(s) who wrote it). The authors are not named here, however, as they are merely contributors. For academic clarity, it is the editor who is recognised as the source. And this is arguably fair as it is usually the editor who initiates the idea, secures the contract with the publisher, and arranges for the book to be written.

We next come to the year of publication, in this case 2018, and then the title of the book which is usually in italics but sometimes underlined. After that, 'London' tells us where it was published and 'Routledge' is the name of the publisher. Routledge is a large, reputable publisher of professional and academic texts, and if you are an eagle-eyed reader you will have noticed that this is also the publisher of the volume you are currently reading. The final item is the ISBN which stands for International Standard Book Number. This is the unique number allocated to that book (Google it and see what hits you get). With all this information, then, librarians can locate the item easily. But it is not just a location tool for librarians. It is also informative and useful for anyone else engaged in an academic inquiry of some sort. Each piece of information serves a purpose for locating the text and/or supporting your engagement with the literature.

There is another key purpose for having a reference list which is arguably even more important than what we have already discussed, and that is the necessity to build on and credit the work of others. Referencing enables you to demonstrate that an idea, model, strategy, figure and so on is the work of another. For instance, suppose you have read that Michel Foucault's ideas promote parallels between schools and societal disciplinarity, as executed in the form of the prison system. And that the use of uniforms, rules, imposed values, surveillance, and time-controlled activities in schools, results in a form of institutional violence, thus functioning in a similar manner to the penal-like environment of a prison. If you have interpreted his work in this way, and decide to use it in your argument, you would need to cite Foucault fully. This is not your idea so you cannot take it and use it out of context as this is a form of stealing. It is literary theft, or plagiarism, and for the most part students who do this do so through naivety. That is, they unintentionally pass off an idea as their own because of academic inexperience. What is needed is clear signposting to where this idea came from – and that is your citation. Scholars deserve credit for their work, and this is no different from visiting the Louvre and seeing the Mona Lisa hanging on the wall with the painter's name (Leonardo da Vinci, in case you are wondering) referenced on a placard at the side. The gallery sees fit to include da Vinci's name so that he can be acknowledged for his contribution to art.

A central purpose for referencing, then, is to acknowledge the source of someone's words, information or ideas and to enable others to track down this source if needed. Let's imagine that you are reading a text and you come across an idea that is perfect for your assignment. The author makes passing reference to it and cites Cerbin (2011). You want to find out more so you head to the reference section. This should help you to locate the source, and today's publications often carry a digital object identifier (DOI). This is a string of letters and numbers that acts as a unique code for a particular item, such as a journal article. In this way the article can be located immediately. According to Paskin (2009, p. 1586), DOIs have 'been developed and implemented in a range of publishing applications since 2000.' This makes your source easily locatable through a simple Google search. Referencing allows you to acknowledge the contributions of other writers and researchers in your field, then, and most written assignments in a university draw on ideas, words or research in this way. By citing the work of a particular scholar, you attribute credit to that person and acknowledge and respect their intellectual property rights. As a mature student, you can draw on any of the millions of ideas, insights and arguments published by other writers, many of whom have spent years researching and writing.

Referencing is also a way to provide evidence to support the assertions and claims in your own assignments. It demonstrates that you are drawing on a validated form of knowledge and that you can navigate your way through it. Citations thus make your writing more persuasive because it means that your work is building on the work of others – you are (metaphorically) standing on the shoulders of giants when referencing. It is important to reference accurately, however, and you can do this by keeping a record of all the sources you use when reading for your assignment. In this way, you should not miss any or find them difficult to locate later on. Indeed, it is extremely frustrating to note down a quote or idea that you want to talk about and then later find that your notes only contain the idea and 'Paskin (2009),' leaving you with no knowledge of who Paskin is and where this source came from. When you are collecting your sources of information and noting down key quotes, then, be sure to record the full citation, or at least the DOI or ISBN, so that you can trace this source again if you need to (see also Chapters 6–8).

▶ WHICH SYSTEM SHOULD I USE?

In your degree, you will be expected to cite the work of others and follow the referencing guidelines of your university. The particular format your institution uses is worth learning as it will help you throughout your study. However, learning how to reference under one particular system can be temporal and, unfortunately, not always readily transferrable as there are many systems available. This might not seem to make sense but there is historical significance within the various disciplines that links reference styles to institutions, and different fields have different styles because they have different purposes. Whilst there is a strong argument and much ambition for establishing a single, Esperanto-like, style, of referencing, this is unlikely to happen for quite some time (if at all).

Learning your university's particular style is worthwhile as you will use it throughout your degree. And you may even decide to continue with your studies in the same university. Familiarising yourself with the referencing format, then, might be a small investment that pays healthy dividends in the coming years. And if you are lucky enough to be working in a field where the referencing has been standardised – e.g. psychology, languages, sciences – learning the referencing system for your studies might also put you in good stead for your career. In general, however, referencing is complex and even styles based on institutions such as 'Harvard' can have multiple versions, depending on the interpretation of each university subscribing to it. Harvard is linked to Harvard University. It provides a set way of referencing, such as alphabetizing the reference list and including the author's name and year of publication for citations (Clauss et al., 2013). To illustrate this, the above Cain reference can be seen below in Harvard form:

> Cain, T. (2018). *Becoming a research-informed school.* Routledge.

The name can be misleading in some respects, however, because institutions that use Harvard may each have slightly different versions.

Other styles, such as Modern Language Association (MLA) and the Chicago style are based on systems in the USA. Respectively, these two are primarily used for language and literature and the humanities, whilst APA refers to the *American Psychological Association and* is used for the field of psychology. *Examples of these can be seen below*:

> [MLA] Cain, Tim. *Becoming a research-informed school*. Routledge, 2018.
> [Chicago] Cain, Tim. *Becoming a research-informed school*. Routledge, 2018.
> [APA] Cain, T. (2018). *Becoming a research-informed school*. Routledge.

These are merely examples, of course, and there are many other styles. Each field will favour a certain type of referencing but for those fields that are varied and work across the styles, it is perhaps useful to adhere to a guide than to attempt to memorise the formatting. In the field of education within social sciences, for instance, many journals have in-house styles and the variance across these means that researchers submitting articles for publication often have to redo the formatting to suit the particular journal. If you compile your reference list by hand, methodically working through each one to ensure it is accurate, this can be laborious. However, in today's society where you no longer have to do everything yourself and AI is on hand, there are programs that can assist you.

▶ AUTOMATED APPROACHES

A useful tool for formatting your references is MyBib (https://www.mybib.com). This is an easy-to-use app that will also find and collate your references for you, creating a ready-made reference list for you to export to the format of your choice. And a major bonus to using this is that there is a free version of it. MyBib enables you to locate an item by simply entering the DOI, ISBN or website. And you can even create your own, should the system struggle to retrieve a hit. The studying world is changing and labour-saving devices are to be welcomed. Of course, some uses of AI cross the boundary of ethical practice in academia, but the landscape is being adapted wherever possible (see Chapter 1). Referencing is an academic skill so consigning this to AI can generate waves of dissent. My own take on this is that you should first understand the referencing process and then if you wish to use AI this will allow you more time to get on with the business of learning new things. But is this use of AI a form of cheating? Well, the jury is out on this at present (Petrusheva & Idrizi, 2023), but the perception from some institutions is that it is not a great deal different from using spellchecker to correct your grammar and spelling.

Where spelling and grammar were once key critical aspects for identifying non-academic, or even sloppy, writing, such automated tools– which are commonly available in Word – have been used for decades (see also Chapter 1). And during this time they have significantly improved the presentation of many students' writing. These are now accepted support tools for studying. Could the same be said for AI in the future? Is ChatGPT the new spellchecker (albeit, with incredibly more sophisticated uses and holding the ability to turn the academic world upside down)? Spellchecking is no longer frowned upon in universities (if anything it is promoted), and arguably it would be silly to lose marks for spelling these days, particularly when you have this technology at your fingertips. This may well be the case some day for other forms of AI. For now, however, we shall return to the system of referencing and explore some practical examples for writing.

▶ IN-TEXT REFERENCING

The following references are examples of how you can cite the literature within the main body of your writing. In the first one, we see that the author, whom I shall cite in this paragraph to avoid confusion – Jones, 2011, p. 3 – uses her citation to support what she is arguing but states her point in her own voice:

> For those entering university from foundation courses there is believed to be a mismatch between expectations of skills and what is expected of students by lecturers (Stevenson & O'Keefe, 2011) but this may also apply to those arriving directly from school.

Jones appears to be using her citation of Stevenson & O'Keefe in relation to the 'mismatch' she speaks of. As such, you will notice that she embeds her citation halfway through the sentence. This is worthy of note because it can be a confusing point. Some may choose to place the citation at the end of the sentence, regardless of what it refers to, because that is where they are used to seeing citations. However, it must be noted that that is not necessarily where it belongs. For clarity, a citation should sit comfortably near the statement or idea it relates to. At the end of a sentence may be where you mostly find a citation, but that is because writers often end a sentence with the conclusion of a particular thought or use a citation to support that sentence. In this example, the citation would not work if it was moved to the end as it would read as if it was supporting evidence for the final part of the sentence: 'this may also apply to those arriving directly from school' (Jones, 2011, p. 3). Note the change in focus between this part of the sentence and the first and decide for yourself where the citation is alluding to.

The second example, from Biwer et al. (2023, p. 354), is also an in-text citation:

> Mental effort refers to the amount of resources devoted by the learner to manage task demands.
> (Paas et al., 1994)

This is one way how citations are typically done – at the end of the sentence and used to prop up the comment or suggestion. The third example (Allan, 2022, p. 42) is slightly different again:

> LS is deemed an important tool for student teachers as it engenders the synthesis of critical thinking and practical experience, and thus impacts on "their pedagogical thinking, their knowledge of students, and their teaching practices".
> (Cerbin, 2011, p. 126)

The location of the citation in this is positioned at the end but more accurately you will notice that it is positioned in relation to the direct quote that it refers to. This passage could also have been rewritten to look like this:

> Cerbin (2011, p. 126) suggests that LS is deemed an important tool for student teachers as it engenders the synthesis of critical thinking and practical experience, and thus impacts on "their pedagogical thinking, their knowledge of students, and their teaching practices."

This can be confusing as it depends on whether the source relates to the first part or not. However, we do know that the citation is linked to the actual quotation because of the quotation marks. These tell us that the author's words are being included so we can assume that the citation with the page number relates to that precise quote. But you can probably appreciate that had the first part of the sentence stated something to the contrary, the positioning of the citation might have been misleading.

The examples above utilise closed-off citations. That is, they draw on the citations as supporting evidence for what is written. In this way, the parentheses separate the citations from the main body of text. But there are other ways to draw on your sources, and sometimes the author is part of your narrative. Consider the following:

> Braun and Clarke's (2006) 6-step guide to conducting TA was followed.
> (Thompson et al., 2021, p. 1400)

Braun and Clarke are not bracketed off from the author's construction because they are part of it. A common mistake in referencing is to adopt this approach yet still close the cited authors off, as can be seen in this erroneous example:

> Braun and Clarke's (2006) 6-step guide to conducting TA was followed.
> (Thompson et al., 2021, p. 1400)

This does not make sense because the sentence here starts with '6-step guide' when it should actually start with 'Braun and Clarke's...'

▶ HOW MANY REFERENCES DO I NEED?

The final point to cover in this chapter is in relation to how many references are needed. This is not an easy question because there is no single right answer, only numerous wrong ones. The magic number is hard to define but as students ask this question so much I think it is only fair to address it here in some manner. Firstly, let's put a ballpark figure on it. A journal article of around 6,000 words might contain between 30 and 50 references on average. So, there you have your figure. You just need to do a simple recalculation. For a 3,000-word assignment, for example, you can half the number of references to 15–25. Now I must advise that you take this only as a guide ('with a pinch of salt'). The number of references really depends on your content and how you use them. Too many references and you sell yourself short and fail to engage with the individual sources in any depth – more is not better. Too few and you are not really providing an overview of the existing understanding. To help you think about the citations you include, Table 9.1 provides some questions and answers.

In the next chapter we will look at some strategies for polishing your work so that you can be content with the finished product and this would be the time to revise those citations.

TABLE 9.1 Questions for including citations

Question	Action
Have I got lots and lots of references that don't really do anything? That is, many studies of the same ilk that are merely shoved inside parentheses with numerous other references also doing the same job?	Consider omitting some of them if they are not doing anything of significance and interact more with your other sources.
Have I engaged deeply with my sources? i.e. have I explored the concepts those studies present, used their arguments to make new meaning, and discussed these in some depth?	Ask yourself, why is this reference here? What purpose does it serve?
Have I used sources that are appropriate for my focus? For example, an investigation into trends in higher education since Covid-19 is unlikely to require many sources pre-2020, but there may be some that are HE-focused and thus tangentially relevant.	Are some references bolted on or do they support your argument?
Are my references valid? That is, are they fit for purpose and do they provide lots of information to move my thinking forward (see also Chapters 6–8)?	Are they current or representative of the current state of the field? Are they robust sources – i.e. peer-reviewed journal articles rather than a random PDF discovered via an Internet search.

▶ REFERENCES

Allan, D. (2022). Lesson study and teacher training: Engaging in the co-construction of pedagogical knowledge. In E. Sengupta, & P. Blessinger (Eds.), *Innovative approaches in pedagogy for higher education classrooms* (1st ed., pp. 41–53). Emerald Publishing Limited.

Biwer, F., Wiradhany, W., Oude Egbrink, M. G. A., & de Bruin, A. B. H. (2023). Understanding effort regulation: Comparing "Pomodoro" breaks and self-regulated breaks. *British Journal of Educational Psychology, 93*(S2). https://doi.org/10.1111/bjep.12593

Braun, V. & Clarke, V. (2006). Using thematic analysis in psychology. *Qualitative Research in Psychology, 3*(2), 77–101. 10.1191/1478088706qp063oa.

Clauss, M., Müller, D. W. H., & Codron, D. (2013). Source references and the scientist's mind-map: Harvard vs. Vancouver style. *Journal of Scholarly Publishing, 44*(3), 274–282. https://doi.org/10.3138/jsp.44.3.005

Cerbin, B. (2011). *Lesson study: Using classroom inquiry to improve teaching and learning in higher education*, First Edition. Routledge.

Jones, H. (2011). Are our students prepared for university? *Bioscience Education*, *18*(1), 1–12. https://doi.org/10.3108/beej.18.3se

Paas, F. G. W. C., van Merriënboer, J. J. G., & Adam, J. J. (1994). Measurement of cognitive load in instructional research. *Perceptual and Motor Skills*, *79*(1), 419–430. https://doi.org/10.2466/pms.1994.79.1.419

Paskin, N. (2009). Digital object identifier (DOI®) system. *Encyclopedia of Library and Information Sciences, Third Edition*, 1586–1592. https://doi.org/10.1081/e-elis3-120044418

Petrusheva, K. M., & Idrizi, E. (2023). AI technologies and learning: Tertiary level students' awareness and perceptions of AI: To what extent are students aware of the opportunities of AI for learning? *International Journal of Education & Philology*, *4*(2), 36–45.

Stevenson, C., & O'Keefe, J. (2011). Developing students' research and inquiry skills from year one: A research informed teaching project from the University of Sunderland. *Innovative Practice in Higher Education*, *1*(1), 1–26.

Thompson, M., Pawson, C., & Evans, B. (2021). Navigating entry into higher education: The transition to independent learning and living. *Journal of Further and Higher Education*, *45*(10), 1398–1410. https://doi.org/10.1080/0309877x.2021.1933400

10 Revising and Polishing Your Writing

▶ INTRODUCTION

Revising your writing can be a laborious undertaking but it is essential for those wishing to exhibit a level of professionalism in their work. As you progress towards establishing prestige in your field, you should pay attention to detail and take pride in what you do. Whatever your profession, any of your written outputs that might enter the public domain or be used in a professional capacity – such as reports, statements, articles, blogs, board papers for institutional meetings, and so on – may be representative of you and your professionalism. This is a skill, therefore, that you can (and should) begin developing through your academic writing at university. You may thoroughly enjoy the process of editing, and revel in the polished writing that is produced from it. Or you may only hold contempt for this seemingly extra workload that you have been subjected to after you have already produced your first draft. But there are definite benefits to be had from revising your work. Firstly, there are few people who can write their best work in one draft. I know of none, but you may have heard rumours. Secondly, you potentially sell yourself short when you do this because you are throwing away a wonderful opportunity to produce something you can be proud of. It is not advisable to rely on your first draft, then, as it rarely results in a work of great literary merit. Of course, you don't have to labour over every point like the following humorous exchange between Oscar Wilde and his friend and biographer suggests:

> **Oscar Wilde:** I was working on the proof of one of my poems all the morning and took out a comma.
> **Robert Sherard:** And in the afternoon?
> **Oscar Wilde:** In the afternoon? Well, I put it back again.
> (Source: Gantar, 2016, p. 35)

However, you do need to exercise an element of care in polishing your work so that it presents you in the greatest light. The written word is a gift in that it can be remoulded and reinvented before it is passed on so you should take advantage of this. You cannot do this with speech and many of us have been in the position where we wish we could rewind time and take back our words, only to think more carefully before choosing alternatives. We can revise our writing, however, and where possible you should evaluate your work, edit it and make any necessary amendments you see fit until you are thoroughly happy that you can release it into the world. To explore this further, let's look at having your assignment marked.

▶ UNDERSTANDING ASSESSMENT CRITERIA

You may wonder what assessment criteria has to do with editing and revising, particularly if you have already written your assignment. But the assessment criteria are the means upon which you will be judged. These guidelines steer the person marking your work towards deciding on a grade. They provide a set of descriptors for each grade and how well you meet these will dictate which category most accurately describes your work. In the assessment criteria, you will see that the language differs for each category, and this is used to differentiate between the grades. The person marking your work will read and apply these criteria as accurately as they can. In the lower categories you will see language such as 'demonstrates some understanding of the literature' whilst for the higher grades the language explicitly illustrates the distinction, with phrases such as 'demonstrates a consistent and systematic understanding of the literature.' The first suggests that the student made some references to the literature but did not, perhaps, conduct a thorough review of it, maybe even leaving out some key texts in the debate or not engaging deeply enough with the sources. In the higher category, a 'systematic understanding' denotes a structured approach and thus consistency throughout. It suggests that the analysis of the literature is robust and that the assignment was coherent. And the term 'consistent' is a key one (look out for it) as it is a significant differentiator. When applied to marking an assignment, it makes a clear distinction between those that only just meet the outcomes (pass) but show potential – e.g. the assignment has just two strong paragraphs where the author engages critically with the literature and illustrates only superficial engagement for the rest of it – and those that are consistent throughout. Some evidence of conducting a high-level analysis and evaluation in some of the assignment is great, but the overall grade is decided as a whole. When revising your work, then, ensure it is consistent throughout. After all, if you can do it once you can do it on multiple occasions.

Consistency is an easy win for both you and the examiner because it is a clear sign that you are in that particular grading bracket. Hitting that category in a partial way shows your examiner that you have the potential – and that will be reflected in your feedback as a developmental point – but it results in your average grade being lower than it might have been. Put yourself in the role of the person marking this. If the examiner can easily see where it needs developing, could you? If you cannot see it this time, use your feedback when revising your next assignment and talk to your tutor.

The final point to mention about assessment relates to the learning outcomes. Whilst the assessment criteria will dictate your grade and how well you meet it from an academic perspective, the achievement of the learning outcomes for the module will be the deciding factor for a pass or fail. You have to meet all the learning outcomes (usually) in order to pass the module so you should ensure that you understand them. If you have followed the advice and written your assignment with those in mind, you are off to a good start. Now return to them and polish your work so you can ensure that you achieved what you set out to do and that it is explicit. Often when we write it does not go to plan, particularly if we become engrossed in the exercise of free writing. It is therefore very important that you return to your draft to ensure that it is doing what you intended it to do. Also, you can rework your draft so that it aligns with your structure. Ask yourself where you went off track, then, and what editing it will take to get you back on it. It may even be the case that your plan is no longer fit for purpose. This is fine and is not unusual because a plan in the early stages is only a loose guide for where you think your assignment will go.

Not everything goes according to plan so it is perhaps more important at this stage for you to revisit your format to ensure that the structure of your assignment is consistent with how it has been written. What story would you like it to tell? One way to do this is to create an overall question. This condenses your focus and maximises your chances of satisfying the learning outcomes. If you already have one – e.g. in the assignment title – that is great. But many assignments have a broad focus and thus you should sharpen yours by devising a suitable question. Your personal tutor can steer you on this in the early stages of your writing, but you can also do it retrospectively as you are editing. That is, ask yourself what you are trying to achieve, and what question you are looking to answer with this assignment. Having a question that could be applied to the assignment will highlight whether you have achieved it or not and will hone your structure. In this way, you demonstrate a coherent format, perhaps along the lines of, 'this is my idea, this is how I approached it, this is what the literature said, this is what I found through my investigation, and this is my contribution and explanation of what it all means.'

▶ EDITING YOUR WORK

We shall now move to the actual mechanics of editing. Suppose you have drafted up your 3,500-word assignment and you are 800 words over. You need to lose 800 words, but you are unsure of how to do this. Firstly, 800 words is not a lot so you should look upon this as not being too onerous. Secondly, there will be some leeway on the word count. This is usually 10%, which is designed to hone your academic ability, but you will need to check your institution's regulations on this as universities differ. In your 3,500-word assignment, then, you have already taken off the leeway of 10% from your draft of 4,650 and you still need to reduce it by another 800 words. This is the time to get tough, to become ruthless with your text. If you are precious about what you have written and unsure of what you can delete, you will need a strategy. One way to do this is to cut out any irrelevant sections. This is where your question comes in, too. Omit anything that does not answer the question or provide context for you to do so. This can reduce your word count significantly, but you do need to ensure that you are still meeting your aim and that you haven't removed anything important. It is possible that your structure has changed and that large sections that you wrote earlier on are now irrelevant. Don't keep them in for the sake of it, or merely because you worked hard in writing them, because in the long run they will bring your grade down.

If you are really precious about your writing, or just that bit unsure whether you have done the right thing in deleting some of it, then I would recommend setting up an archive folder and putting your deleted text into that for safe keeping. After all, there could be something here that is integral to your response to the assignment – perhaps a key discussion that illuminates your whole argument. If you have done a solid job in your editing, however, you should never need to go back to this folder. But it is comforting to know that at just a few clicks you can have all that work instantly returned to your document. There is no harm in this and it gives you peace of mind.

To identify your large sections, go back to your question. What is the thread running through your assignment? Does each section meet the focus of the narrative? Suppose you have written your assignment for your Geography degree on ecosystems and there is a section on geohazards. Originally this was interrelated, but you can now see from your draft that even though there is a connection with the theme, you have not explored this at all. As such, this section of writing does not fit with the overall assignment focus. Your question related to ecosystems, and you have addressed that, but it is now clear that the only way in which you could leave in the geohazards section is to develop it much more and to fully integrate it into the assignment's focus. The word limit does not allow this unless you take out other sections and overhaul the whole assignment. Would taking this section out detract from the overall message? Is it a benefit? Or is your structure more streamlined without it? If the thread running through does not lend itself to a discussion on geohazards then take it out.

In one way, taking out large sections of text is an easy win. In another way, however, you may feel that there is nothing that you can remove that will not have a deleterious effect on your writing. In this situation, all is not lost and you can tighten your work in other ways and still retain the content. In doing so, you do not lose any of the valuable writing that you have done, but your sentences become more succinct. There are two examples of text below and each contains the same purpose and, hopefully, the same message. They are designed to illustrate how you can use revision to become more succinct in your writing, cutting down the verbiage that merely pushes you over your word count. Text A is your first attempt, your draft, and now you need to sharpen it. You have explored the idea of taking out some larger sections, but either nothing appears prominent, or you have done all you can and still have more words to get rid of. So now it is down to the writing itself and you produce Text B. Have a look at the two versions (Texts A & B) of the same message, then, and see if you can identify what has changed. This will be discussed in more detail below.

Text A

This project seeks to explore the nature of alternative provision (AP) for secondary schools and is aimed at pupils aged between 11 and 16 years old, studying in non-mainstream schools in England as an alternative to their compulsory education. Through an in-depth exercise in mapping out the nature of this diverse provision, including the variety of different approaches to teaching and learning that many of these settings use, this project will highlight the ways in which this sector makes positive contributions to the lives of young people who, for a wide variety of reasons, are not able to access, or have failed to flourish, in mainstream school environments. This project, therefore, will seek to undertake research with schools in the education division of Improving Participation Group (IPG) – an organisational allegiance with an innovative business model that is heavily committed to impacting on, changing, and improving, young people's lives during their compulsory education years. Improving Participation Group states that its key purpose is to provide access to bespoke, alternative education environments with high-quality teaching and learning, and employment advice and guidance as well as many networking opportunities through its extensive partnership. This project will therefore investigate and evaluate the many ways in which each learning environment, and its individual approach to meeting young people's needs, strives to ensure a tailored and productive pathway of learning for all its students. It is envisaged that the main aim will be to explore some of the many barriers to engagement that the students have previously experienced, and to identify a wide range of successful strategies that are currently being implemented for students in alternative provision. The methodology will enable the capture of data through a wide variety of quantitative and qualitative methods. The project promotes the examination of various pedagogical innovations that teachers employ when designing and delivering learning for previously disengaged students. This project, then, will be used to develop a research-informed pedagogy that can shape the future teaching and the learning experiences of many potentially disadvantaged young people.

336 words

Text B
This project explores the nature of alternative provision (AP) in education for pupils aged 11–16 years in non-mainstream schools in England. By mapping the nature of this diverse provision, and the different approaches to teaching and learning that many of these settings use, it will highlight the ways in which this sector makes positive contributions to the lives of young people who, for a variety of reasons, are not able to access, or have failed to flourish, in mainstream schooling. This project will undertake research with schools in the education division of Improving Participation Group (IPG) – a business committed to impacting on young people's lives through providing access to high-quality alternative education and career support. It will investigate the ways in which teaching and learning in AP meets the needs of students within IPG settings. The aims of the project are to explore some of the barriers to engagement in learning, to examine pedagogical innovations for disengaged students, and to develop a research-informed pedagogy for the wider AP sector.

170 words

The two texts have the same aim and, arguably, deliver the same message. You may feel that the second is sharper, however, and more succinct. It enables the writer to lose 166 words from this one section alone. And whilst 166 words may not sound much in the grand scheme of things, we should bear in mind the shortness of the original section at just 360 words. If applied across your whole assignment this would have a significant effect as Text B contains around half the number of words as Text A. This suggests that you can edit your work without losing the original message. However, you may feel that Text B is a little too short and that even though it has been sharpened in many respects, and is now punchier, the language has lost some off its richness. This is fine as you can revisit it and either rebuild it or return to a copy of the original. It is thus a good idea to have back-up copies of your assignment at several stages of your writing. This will enable you to return to an earlier draft if your editing becomes a little too enthusiastic, and having several versions provides evidence for you to look back on and analyse the process of editing. How successful was it? What could have been done better?

Moreover, you never know when that hard drive will collapse or the cloud will become unavailable for a period of time (usually at a crucial point near your submission deadline) as the system undergoes an update. You can go back to the original, then, or any particular version along the editing journey, and revise it accordingly. When making changes to your text, think about how you have used your words and your sentence structure overall. You will notice from the texts that the first line is different on each so from the outset there are changes happening. Here are the sentences again with the key changes underlined. Look at them closely:

Text A
This project <u>seeks to</u>[1] explore the nature of alternative provision (AP) <u>for secondary schools</u>[2] and <u>is aimed at</u>[3] pupils aged between 11 and 16 years old, <u>studying</u>[4] in non-mainstream schools in England <u>as an alternative to their compulsory education.</u>[5]

Text B
This project explores the nature of alternative provision (AP) in education for pupils aged 11–16 years in non-mainstream schools in England.

Text A is tentative whilst Text B is more committed. Also, Text B is more succinct – stating the same thing in a shorter amount of words – and the duplication has been removed. Overall, the five changes identified are elaborated on below:

1) We do not need 'seeks to' when we can turn 'explore' into 'explores.' This does a very similar job.
2) We do not need to be told that it is 'for secondary schools' when we will also be informed that these are 'pupils aged between 11 and 16 years old' in 'schools in England.' An alternative might be

to say 'all pupils in secondary schools' and remove the qualifier as the focus is not on a specific age range.
3) The use of the word 'for' results in the phrase 'is aimed at' becoming redundant. And in Text A we have both.
4) 'Studying' is superfluous as these are young people in compulsory education and thus studying is the purpose of their presence there.
5) We know from the first line that the subject is alternative provision. Therefore, 'as an alternative to their compulsory education' also becomes redundant.

You can continue the microanalysis on the text to establish why the changes were made and, as already mentioned, you may not agree with all of them. But hopefully the purpose of the exercise is clear in that drafts of our writing can often be revised for both clarity and brevity. Once you have cut your work down, do remember to read over it again. What might seem to make sense in the midst of editing might not be clear at all when you reread the text as a whole. And there may even be a small job to do in revisiting the structure. Does it still make sense and is it coherent? Is there a sequential flow to the narrative? One of the common attributes of a low-graded assignment – which is usually a sign that the student did not do enough work and tried to chance their luck – is the inclusion of lots of free writing and reams and reams of waffle. This should be avoided at all costs and is usually related to poor time management (see Chapter 3). In order to be clear about what you are trying to achieve in your writing, you have to be ruthless in your editing and what I like to call the Hollywood approach can help you to get your head around how this can be done.

▶ THE HOLLYWOOD APPROACH

To understand the Hollywood analogy, first think about your favourite Hollywood film (if you have one) and then consider the writing that it took to produce that end product. Everything that happens in that film will have been carefully crafted and there will be no wasted lines. If a character mumbles it is because that is a trait of that person, whilst if another receives a utility bill and shoves it in the drawer there will be a reason for doing so. It might not be clear at the time, but an analysis of the film will show that it had a purpose. Whilst some lines may be thrown away by an individual actor, these are not written as such. Every line counts and every shot is meaningful. Let's look at a fictitious example: Anne Hathaway crosses the street and a taxi slows down as the driver beeps the horn. We see that the character driving is wearing a dark uniform, but we don't really see his face. It is just an average yellow taxi. Denzel Washington watches Anne from the other side of the street. He is looking mysterious and suspicious. Is he following her?

We dismiss the taxi incident because it was minor and seems meaningless – it is just something that happened, a part of everyday life. The taxi came close but it did not hit her so we think nothing more of it. Or perhaps we feel that this behaviour is a reflection of her character – is she struggling at the moment, does it represent her confusion and poor state of mind at the time of crossing? We later see that 'suspicious' Denzel is actually a detective and not so suspicious. He has been hired to follow Anne and look out for her wellbeing, so we join the dots and revise our original opinion of him to believe he does not have nefarious intentions. Later still, the taxi is seen again and now we see the driver with a threatening look on his face, and as the camera pans down it reveals a gun on the passenger seat. The seemingly meaningless moment of earlier now holds much significance and we realise that the driver was following Anne, perhaps looking to bump her off.

The point of the above analogy is to encourage you to think like a scriptwriter when revising your writing and crafting your assignments. What is in there that does not need to be there? In the Hollywood film example, events that seem meaningless will have meaning later on, and anything that did not need to be in the script has already been edited out. Professional writers ask themselves, how is this particular line moving the narrative forward or providing insight into the character? What is the purpose of this section? Why is this character here, and why did she say that? If there isn't a purpose, it is usually removed. We all know that huge sections of films have ended up on the cutting room floor, and many have alternative versions – the director's cut, for instance. Decisions are made on the content and everything within reason must be justified. This might not feel like it when you are watching a film that you find is slow for the first 30 minutes, but those decisions, whether rightly or wrongly, have been made along the way. Conducting such a micro-analysis on your work will help you enormously as it will enable you to write much better and to revise what you have written so that it is tighter and sharper. Be ruthless in your editing, then, and take it out if it does not contribute to your aim. You can have your 'Director's cut' (a back-up copy or a folder containing the deleted text) but the version that is submitted must be the best you can possibly make it. You are now honing your work in the way that a professional would and (hopefully) well on your way to (re)writing that brilliant assignment.

In the final chapter of this book we will look at the role of the personal tutor in helping you to reconceptualise your degree experience as an opportunity for both personal and professional growth in academia, and thus preparation for working in your chosen career.

▶ REFERENCE

Gantar, J. (2016). *The evolution of Wilde's wit*. Springer.

11 Making the Most of Your Personal Tutor

▶ INTRODUCTION

From the beginning of your learning journey, it is likely that you will need someone to guide you through the process of surviving and thriving in HE, outlining what will be expected of you and supporting you in your every need. Even as a mature student, whether you are only slightly older than your peers or have many decades of life experience, you should never feel that you are alone, particularly when unsupported and unprepared mature students have a higher tendency of dropping out of HE altogether (Bolam & Dodgson, 2003). We all need a little help from time to time and that is exactly what your personal tutor (PT) is there for. Your PT also knows the university, is familiar with the online systems, and how the modules run, and understands the transition into full-time study. As such, your PT may even be on hand to recommend other forms of support as well. This can save you a lot of time and effort. You are not expected to know everything, regardless of what you may have done previously, because this is a new environment that presents new challenges. And of course, you may be ahead of the game when dealing with things that come your way and confident that events will eventually turn out well; that is, you have enough resilience and experience to face the challenges ahead (see Chapter 1). But there are always people on hand to support you so even though you are developing your autonomy, you are never fully alone. It is useful, then, to have an insight into the type of support that is available and what to expect from your PT. The first step for your PT is to organise a meeting early in your studies, preferably in the first (induction) week. This might be an informal meeting, but it immediately gives you a point of call for any questions you have. And if your PT cannot directly help you, they will be able to signpost you to the relevant service.

▶ THE QUALITIES OF A PT

The qualities of a PT are important for student success and a study by Elyse Wakelin in 2021 found that personal tutoring difficulties amounted to the following three areas:

1. Confusion and ambiguity in the role of the PT
2. PTs demonstrating a lack of confidence and awareness of the purpose of their role
3. Poorly focused tutorials (Wakelin, 2021).

We shall thus address these in this chapter.

Your PT is usually, but not always, your first port of call. It is the person you go to to resolve a concern (although a module leader might be better placed if it relates to a specific module). Your PT understands your personal circumstances and can provide advice and guidance on things beyond mere assignments. Whether it is settling into your new campus accommodation, arranging a parking permit for your car, or helping you to manage your workload, your PT can be there for you – encouraging you to succeed and addressing your queries. S/he is non-judgemental and can support you with personal difficulties as well as provide you with academic support. In this way, you may learn more from your PT when you start your course but become more autonomous, and thus less reliant on your PT, once you are up and running and aware of how things function in the university. Your PT may take on a different approach at this point, however, focusing more on academic guidance to get you through your assignments. But your PT is also on hand should you begin to flounder in the mire of university life. Good PTs understand your individual needs, can recognise when you are in need of reassurance or are genuinely struggling, and can help you to establish some solid plans for getting back on track. It is important to know how to use your PT, then, for maximum effect. To do this, let's look at who your PT might be.

A good PT will be an established academic or at least be very experienced in the world in which you are operating. This means that your PT is in many ways a role model who can guide you to similar success. Of course, your goal may not be to actually become an academic one day. But you will need to engage in academic life for the duration of your degree. And there is much commonality in the roles of mature student and academic in this respect (Chapman, 2013). You are learning to function in an academic world so who else is in a better position to support that journey than someone already in that world? Your PT has also (hopefully) been to university, has achieved well academically, and knows how to thrive in this area. But you are not looking to merely mimic that person; rather, you should hope to learn from their experience and subsequently use your time effectively to become a better scholar and to avoid making unnecessary mistakes.

In addition to academic support, your PT may also be experienced in the same field as the one you are looking to enter. If you are studying engineering, for instance, or law, your PT may be a former engineer or an ex-lawyer. Moreover, many lecturers also maintain links with their previous professions – e.g. drama tutors working as semi-professional actors, musicians agreeing to do the odd gig, and nurses signed up as bank staff to work some shifts around their teaching. This gives them real-world experience that is current and extremely valuable. They may even signpost you to some paid employment as well (but don't expect this). In this situation, you almost certainly want to engage in conversations about real-life working environments and listen to some of their potentially fascinating tales of working in the field. If you are looking to work as a professional actor, for instance, and your PT is currently doing this, this is a marvellous opportunity to get to understand the current climate (and possibly do some networking). This insight is incredibly useful for your profession and could save you a lot of time and effort in the long run.

Some lecturers will engage in their former profession for a number of reasons, the prime ones being that they can earn extra money, can continue doing something that they love, and can remain current within their profession. This ensures their teaching is relevant and up to date and may even provide a route back into the profession should they wish to have a career U-turn. Other ways in which your lecturers will sustain their currency may be in the form of research and other scholarly activities. Learning is an ongoing process and fields of study grow and change. A teacher educator may have completed 25 years in a school but if they have been out of their sector for more than five years, and they have not kept up to date with policy changes and new thinking, then they are merely relying on an existing skillset and knowledge that could be obsolete. Good teacher educators will be engaged in scholarly activity to continue their professional learning or may have stints where they return to teach in the relevant sector – e.g. in a primary school.

▶ TUTORIALS

Your first tutorial may be a group one. This is often done deliberately and actually makes sense once you understand why. At this stage in your studies, you and your peers are likely to have very similar needs. Any queries that an individual raises are probably of benefit for the whole group. A group tutorial also enables you to bond with others, to get to know the personalities of your peers and perhaps to see who could be good to collaborate with. Which of your peers has similar interests? Are there other mature students there that you can talk to and what are their experiences? Some may be shy and reserved and say little (or nothing) in that session whilst others may demand more than their fair share of vocal time. Primarily, however, you will see that your peers have similar fears and apprehensions to your own. This should be reassuring and help you stave off that imposer syndrome (which is actually far more common that you might imagine). Of course, much socialising may have already taken place online before you arrived at the university, but seeing and talking to people in person is different enough to count as a new experience.

A strategy that is typically employed by university staff is to bring in second- or third-year students to talk to you about their experiences and provide you with an insight into the university. Some even offer mentorships that you can access over the coming term. Talking to these students can allay any fears you might have, and as they are currently undertaking the same student journey that you are about to embark on, their advice should be relevant and meaningful. As a mature student, you may even be able to draw on your own experiences to support others (see Chapter 1), and this will help you to bond with your peers. If you have a lot of interesting life experience, for instance, don't hide it in order to seemingly fit in. Utilise it as it is a strength. After all, this is what the students around you will want when they graduate. Imagine, for instance, that you have worked in an office for many years beforehand and a peer asks a question about a potential hazard in a building. Drawing on your experience from your previous role, you decide to interject and talk about hazards, and you even relay some real-life scenarios. Your new peers are intrigued as you strengthen your relationship with them and perhaps even make new friends. This is important because, like everyone around you, you may feel a little vulnerable. Using your experience in this way is empowering. A group tutorial is thus useful for situating yourself and your peers together within the context of the university. As you relate to your peers, it can be reassuring to discover that you are not alone in your thoughts and that you have an opportunity to share your experiences and bond accordingly.

Planning

In your first individual tutorial, your PT will no doubt want to plan your year out in relation to your potential needs. However, s/he will not be responsible for writing up a schedule for you that includes all your deadlines. This you will need to do for yourself, and it is great exercise in autonomy (another area where being a mature student might give you an advantage). Your PT will mostly concentrate on when your tutorials will be and will ask you to consider key dates so s/he may provide some advice on planning. What you are looking for at this stage is to have an overview of how your year will look. In this way, there are not likely to be any surprise expectations. However, should something unforeseeable arise that needs dealing with, your plan will enable you to have both the time and the intellectual capacity to deal with it strategically. When composing your plan (see also Chapter 3), first identify your assessment points and all the key dates that you need to be aware of. Then, there may be other blocks of time that you need to account for – e.g. what holidays are there? Are you expected to be on a placement or undertaking a particular activity at some period across the year? Events such as placements can eat into your time, so you want to ensure that you have plenty of time for preparation for your assignments. This planning is discussed in full, and with examples given, in Chapter 3.

Your PT will also want to plan your PT sessions together (tutorials). It is common to have between 3 and 5 of these per year, although this will vary from institution to institution. Your PT will have an idea of the content to be covered in each tutorial and Table 11.1 provides an example of what this could look like in your first year.

Extra support

In addition to the above, you may even need more tutorials, depending on what else is going on in your life. For instance, suppose you are in the process of writing your assignment and your manager at the local supermarket has also asked you to work extra

TABLE 11.1 Personal tutorial schedule

Tutorial number	Content for conversation
1 (Induction week)	- Introduction to PT and PT role - Access for uni systems, logon details etc. - Settling in - Learning needs - Student Union
2 (Mid-Oct)	- Campus facilities - Attendance and progress - Autumn term expectations - Assignments – planning and submission process, plagiarism etc. - Academic targets - Student support plan (if relevant) - Relevant support services - Library access - General concerns - Organisation and self-management
3 (Mid-Jan)	- Reflections on progress since September - Assignment feedback - Targets for Spring term (may be based on the above feedback) - Academic support - Revisit student support plan
4 (Mid-March)	- Reflections on previous term - Review of targets - Assignment progress - Reminder of assessment processes and support (e.g. late submissions, extensions, policy on mitigating circumstances) - Concerns
5 (Mid-June)	- Reflections on the academic year - Progress update – grades and outstanding assignments - Module options for following year - Plans for the summer - Accommodation arrangements - Career plans

shifts that month. You decide to say yes because you need the money, but you know it will only make it more difficult for you to manage your time. Your PT can help in this situation by providing advice on time management and whether your situation merits an extension or perhaps some bespoke support for academic writing. Whilst the mere offer of undertaking extra shifts is no justification for an extension (you have a responsibility to manage your own time, of course, and your PT is only there to support you), you may also have other concerns in your life – a tragic piece of news, for example, or a sudden illness. In this situation you need to submit an application to the university to have your irregular circumstances officially recorded so that they do not impact on your ability to do your best. This should help to mitigate any detrimental effects that your irregular circumstances are having on your studies and will allow you to achieve the grade that you would have done had that concern never arisen. This might result in an extension and the university will need to evaluate any potentially mitigating circumstances in case further support is needed. You should therefore discuss anything like this with your tutor.

Your responsibilities

Even if you need extra support, you will still have responsibilities as a student. First, you should engage with your tutorials and interact with your PT. It is not solely down to your PT to arrange this, there is a shared responsibility when it comes to tutorial support. Your PT is there for you but you have to be independent and autonomous as well. This might require you to be proactive. That is, don't wait for your PT to get in touch for your second and third tutorials if you have not designed a schedule for the year. You can (and should) contact your PT first to request a date for a tutorial. This is *your* learning journey and you need to demonstrate autonomy where possible. Moreover, a good PT will embrace this approach as that person will also want you to succeed.

▶ MAINTAIN A POSITIVE AND HEALTHY RELATIONSHIP

It is important for you (and your PT) to be clear about the professional boundaries needed to make this relationship work. This does not mean that you have to be distant with your PT, of course.

But turning up at their house one evening for dinner may be a step too far. Your PT is there to get the best out of you but there needs to be professional boundaries. For instance, disclosures made to a PT should be acted upon in the same way as any other working professional, such as a teacher, and some disclosures will not remain solely between the PT and the student. That is, any disclosure to the PT of illegal activity or threat or harm to an individual (particularly if this individual is a minor or deemed to be vulnerable) will be passed on to the relevant authority. This is an extreme example, of course, but its explicitness enables the professional boundaries to be firmly visible. In a more diluted example, we can see that it is easy to cross these boundaries. And whilst there is no harm intended, it is necessary for you as a student to respect them. Late-night emails, for instance, are not appropriate and texts suggest an even closer – and potentially dangerous – relationship. Some PTs will also disagree with engaging in a WhatsApp or Facebook group unless it is an official one and this is both understandable and advisable. In the modern world we live in, academics receive emails on their phones and engage in social media in the evenings. This is mostly done to promote their professional image, but it can be unintentionally abused. If you find your relationship is veering down any of these avenues, do stop and reflect on the situation. You want your PT to be there for you personally and academically, but you also need for that relationship to be professional. Not many people set out to act inappropriately or unprofessionally, of course. In today's world of social media and extensive networking opportunities, however, it is easy to cross the line when the boundaries are blurred. This protects your interests as well.

But it is not all doom and gloom, of course, and you should have a healthy and long-lasting relationship with your PT that may even go beyond your studies. A good PT will enable you to fulfil your goals and thus thoroughly enjoy your degree experience. Your PT can also advise on employment opportunities and act as a referee for you. As such, it is likely that you will speak affectionately about this time in your life for many years after you have graduated. My own former students (some from over a decade ago) still drop an email to me at times to let me know how they are getting on or ask my advice. And it is great to see that many have thrived in both the private and the public sector. So, do set out on a good footing with your PT and hopefully you will maintain a productive and long-term relationship with him/her. Most importantly, you should remember that your PT wishes you to succeed as much as you do. Do embrace the support, therefore, and you can really make your degree pay off.

▶ REFERENCES

Bolam, H., & Dodgson, R. (2003). Retaining and supporting mature students in higher education. *Journal of Adult and Continuing Education*, *8*(2), 179–194. https://doi.org/10.7227/jace.8.2.5

Chapman, A. (2013). A (re)negotiation of identity: From "mature student" to "novice academic". *Widening Participation and Lifelong Learning*, *14*(3), 44–61. https://doi.org/10.5456/wpll.14.3.44

Wakelin, E. (2021). Personal tutoring in higher education: An action research project on how improve personal tutoring for both staff and students. *Educational Action Research*, *31*(5), 1–16. https://doi.org/10.1080/09650792.2021.2013912

12 Bon Voyage

▶ THE NEXT STEPS

We began the discussion of study skills in this book with a look at your existing potential through a SWOT analysis exercise (see Chapter 1), identifying your current skillset and experience. This is important because it is likely that you already have a lot of experience that you can draw on as you learn new skills. For instance, academic writing may not be your strong point, but if you are a committed and self-motivated individual, who sees things through and is keen to embrace new challenges, you can make the most of these qualities to help you improve. As you probably know, to become proficient at something you often need to work at it, and this requires commitment (and arguably motivation if you are to sustain that commitment). Seeing the bigger picture also helps because you can learn to overcome obstacles, conceptualising them as temporary setbacks, and then plan for progression beyond these. This is why your existing skills and experience can support you, even if it is just in your outlook. They will not carry you through academia, of course, and there is a lot to learn as a new student, but they will hopefully help you to focus and achieve.

If you have arrived at this chapter having undergone all the preceding ones and have worked hard in developing those areas, you are to be commended. In this case, your next steps are designed to build on these areas, and you should continue developing as you enter your chosen profession. To support this process, your SWOT analysis can become your SWOT CV. That is, you can use your CV (résumé) to identify the academic skills and areas of professional experience that you would like to strengthen. Ask yourself what you would like (need) to see on your CV and then use this information to seek ways to acquire this experience. In this way, your CV is not just a collation of your existing skillset and experience, it also facilitates further development.

In many ways, then, the process is cyclical, and even in your first year of studying you should be thinking about your future and where you want your degree to take you. It is never too early to plan for what is in store for you beyond graduation, particularly as many of the skills that you will need for employment in your chosen career will have been acquired throughout the whole of your degree course. As recommended earlier, this means that you should develop and monitor your skills from the outset, evaluating their usefulness for your future profession and, where possible, updating your CV so that you have an account of these experiences.

▶ FINAL THOUGHTS

A degree can be individually fulfilling and bring numerous developmental rewards to you as a person, as well as holding potential to facilitate greater financial returns. A degree can help you to build your autonomy and become more independent in your outlook. It can also enable you to become a better problem solver in general by encouraging you to be critical and analytical, thus guiding you towards reaching your own solutions when faced with life's challenges. Most of all, however, you should aim to enjoy the experience. Many people look back on their university study with fondness, revelling in the nostalgia and appreciating the opportunities it has afforded them, and hopefully you too will engage in this act. Prepare for your journey, then, invest some time in acquiring the skills and abilities (as outlined in this book) that you need to succeed, observe yourself as you progress, and then engage in self-reflection to see how much you have grown.

We should finish this book on a positive note because doing a degree as a mature student is a wonderful experience that can be life changing. This is not goodbye, then, but, as the chapter title suggests, a wish for you to enjoy the journey ahead. Your university study is an opportunity for you to make that career change work, follow your dreams, and become the person you wish to be. This is not a cliché, however. It is a highly plausible outcome, and thousands of mature students demonstrate this every year. Obviously, you will also want your studying to be successful. But, like most things in life, this will not happen easily, and it is likely that you are already giving up a lot to make this change in your life. Therefore, you should go forth with your studies with your eyes fully open. Undertaking a degree, particularly as a mature student, can appear daunting at first and may even seem like an impossibility when you consider how this extra workload will fit into your existing lifestyle and commitments. And to say that it is an easy road to travel is perhaps misleading. It requires hard work, commitment and perseverance and, to some extent, small sacrifices. But even though the journey ahead is hard, it is definitely achievable. And it is also a highly rewarding and enjoyable one for most people. Gaps in skills should not be perceived negatively but identified as essential factors to address for your academic progression. They are small steps that will get you to where you want to be. So even though it may seem like you are climbing a hill at present, rest assured that the view from the top is breathtaking.

Index

Pages in *italics* refer to figures and pages in **bold** refer to tables.

academic conventions 10, 61, 108, 111, 120; *see also* academic misconduct; plagiarism
academic misconduct 75
Academic Phrasebank 117
American Psychological Association (APA) 125; *see also* referencing
anxiety 13, 19, 25, 63
argumentation 9, 11, 25–26, 48, 52, 64, 68, 76, 83, 108–118; constructing 52, 64, 68, 87, 90, 93–106; countering 9, 48, 76, 90, 100–105; defending 61, 90, 99; defining 93; evidence 48, 89, **95**, 105–106, 108–110, **110**, 118, **130**; models of 114–117; *see also* debating
artificial intelligence (AI) 9–11, 125–126
aspirations 3–4, 54, 103
assessments 28, *30*, 42, 47–48, 52, 73–75, 110, 133; criteria 133–135; planning for 149, **150**
assignments 2, 4, 6, 8–10, 19–22, 24–25, 29–31, 37–38, 41–48, 52–56, 60–61, 64, 68, 71–74, 79–80, 85–87, 110–113, 118–123, 145–146; editing of 136–143; planning for 149, **150**; writing of 129–143; *see also* assessments
autonomy 3, 48–61, 77, 145, 149–151, 155

barriers to learning *see* obstacles
bias 97–98, 100, 108, **110**; in research 48, 95; *see also* argumentation; worldviews
biochemistry 66
biology 82
brain 41, *72*, 74; brain gym *see* learning myths; decluttering 21; endorphins 23
burnout 22, 37–38, 40; *see also* study-work balance

Cain, T. 121–125
Cambridge English Dictionary 121
cancel culture 100
challenge 5, 7–9, 12, 15, 48–49, 63, 76, 83–84, 100, 114, 144–145, 154; and negative thinking 14
ChatGPT 11, 126; *see also* artificial intelligence
Chicago manual of style 125; *see also* referencing
citations 75–76, 109, 122–129, **130**
classroom practices 6–8, 21
cognition 3, 11; cognitive dissonance 65–69; cognitive load 73; metacognition 3; processing 23
commitment 1–4, 12, 15, 22, 34–39, 49, 53, 56, 154–156; *see also* motivation; study-work balance
computer science 27–28
confidence **4**, 9, 12, 14–15, 47, 52, 71, 93, 96, 99, 105, 108, 118, 145
Covid-19 115, **130**
criticality and critical thinking 5, 8–11, 21, 48, 52, 76–80, 82–91, 94, 104, 113, 118, 125, 128, 134
culture 91, 100
curriculum vitae (CV) 155
cyber-attacks 31

158 Index

debating 3, 5–8, 11, 84, 90, 93, 96, 100–106, 134
debt *see* finances
depression, alleviation of 22
digital object identifier (DOI) 123

editing 31, **44–45**, **72**; journals 83–84, 115, 121, 132–143; *see also* writing
efficiency 15, 42
employers 5, **95**
endorphins *see* brain
engineering 54
environment 5, 20, 26, 42, 63, 138, 144, 147
exams 25–28
exercise 23
experience, lived 1, 4–6, 11–13, 33, 50–51, 58, 60–61

fears 9, 12–15, 28, 55, 148; in education 77; *see also* anxiety
file management 28–32, **72**, 140
finances **4**, 12, 59, 155
Foucault, M. 122

goals 3, 11, 14–15, 18, 28, 47, 50–54, 74, 146, 152
Google Scholar 85–86, 97

habitual behaviour 12; study habits 14–15, 49, 74
Hamlet 90, 116
history *30*, 59
Hollywood approach 141–143
hurdles 52, 58–60

impostor syndrome 12
in-class activities *see* classroom practices
independent learning 6, 9, 13, 18–19, 35, 49–61, 69, 85, 111, 113, 151, 155; *see also* autonomy
insomnia 20
instinct 41, 76
ISBN (International Standard Book Number) 121–125

journals *see* resources

learning: myths 88; outcomes 113, 118, 134–135; *see also* habitual behaviour
lectures 6–7, **36**, 62–64, 67–71, **72**, 73–80
leisure time 21–22, 35, **36**, 37–42, **43–45**
library *see* resources
lifestyle 156
literature 11–12, 28, 60; finding 60, 85–88, 123, **130**; grey literature *30*, 88; reviewing *30*, 47, *70*, 82–91, **95**, 105, 114, 117–118, 134–135; snowballing 86–87; utilising 87, 108–109, **110**, 122, 126–129, **130**
living expenses 34; *see also* finances

Marx, K. 90
massive open online courses (MOOCs) **4**, 9
maths 21, 27, 54
memory 3, 108
mental health 14, 21
mentoring 148
mind clutter 21, 29
mindset theory 20, 22, 96
Modern Language Association 125; *see also* referencing
motivation 12, 20, 22–23, 39, 51–56, 66, 69, 90, 99, 154; self **4**, 154
MyBib 125–126

needs 8, 26, 28, 138, 146–149, **150**; *see also* SWOT analysis
note-taking: and memory 68, 74; electronically **72**; longhand 71, **72**; shorthand 80; strategies 68–69

obstacles 14, 154
Office for Students 1
organisation skills 33–48

paradigms *see* worldviews
Paxman, J., 105
personal tutor 8, 25, 97, 144–153
physical activity *see* exercise
plagiarism 10, 28, 75, **150**; *see also* academic misconduct
planning 2–3, 33, 35, 37–38, **43**, 49–60, 108, 135, 146, 149–151, 154–155; termly 42–48; *see also* time management
point, evidence, explain 94, **95**
policy **44**, 88, 147, **150**
politics 77, 96, 100–105; *see also* argumentation
Pomodoro technique 23–25
preparation, pre-university 13
productivity *see* efficiency
Psychinfo 85
psychology 65–66, 69, 90, 124–125
publication process 83–85, 96–97, 121–124
PubMed 85

quotations 10, 48, **72**, 76, 90, 114–117, 123, 128; *see also* citations

reading lists 13, 85, 97
referencing 114–118, 120–130, **130**; *see also* citations
reflection 34–35, **43**, 58, 67–68, 73–74, 78–79, 97, 116, **150**, 152, 156; models of 67
resources: blogs 84, 132; books 19–24, 75, 79, 83; journals 19–20, 61, 75, 77, 82–85, 97, 123–125, 129, **130**; library 20, 85, 97, **150**; online 20, 24, 47, 84–85, 100–103, 105, 108, 111–112, 144
role models, for academic routes 146
routine 14, 33–35, 40–42; *see also* habitual behaviour
Routledge 121, 124–125

saving your work *see* file management
schedule 25, 34–40; constructing 35–39, 149, **150**, 151; *see also* planning
Schön, D.A. 67
self: analysis 4, 33; awareness 49; control 23, 33, 49; determinism 90; development 11; esteem **4**, 12; motivation **4**, 39, 51, 154; self-governance 33, **150**; study 6; *see also* autonomy; time management
seminars 7, **36**
Shakespeare, W. 90–91, 116–117
sleep 34–35, 116
social media 24, 94, **95**, 98, 152
sociology 54
straw man argument 101–103; *see also* argumentation
stress 22–23, 25, 28, 30, 35, 46, 66
studying: study space 19–22; study-work balance 13–28, 34–35, **36**; *see also* burnout
SWOT analysis (strengths, weaknesses, opportunities, and threats) **4**, 5, 154–155; *see also* CV

technology 19, 46, 54, **72**
time management 12, 20, 32–48, 141, **150**
timetable 34–35, **36**, 37–42, 47
Toulmin model 114
tutorials 8, 145, 147–149, **150**, 151; *see also* personal tutor

University of Manchester *see* Academic Phrasebank

Wilde, O. 82, 133
woke 100
workshops 7
worldviews 97–98; *see also* argumentation

For Product Safety Concerns and Information please contact our EU representative GPSR@taylorandfrancis.com
Taylor & Francis Verlag GmbH, Kaufingerstraße 24, 80331 München, Germany

www.ingramcontent.com/pod-product-compliance
Lightning Source LLC
Chambersburg PA
CBHW050907160426
43194CB00011B/2321